This is a book for every youth pastor or youth ministry volunteer who has ever felt like a little bit of a failure. (Don't worry. You're in good company.)

But this book is especially for the hundreds of youth workers who risked shame and ridicule (and possibly future employment) in order to contribute their stories to this book. Thanks for letting us laugh with you. You're the true heroes.

YOUTH MINISTRY

FAILS

*A Collection of True Stories
from Real Youth Pastors*

INTRODUCTION

This book started with a Facebook post.

Last year, we posted a just-for-fun question in the Stuff You Can Use youth ministry Facebook group. The prompt was simple: "Tell us your biggest youth ministry fail."

For the next week, hundreds of youth pastors and youth ministry volunteers joined the conversation to tell some of their most horrible, humiliating, and hilarious stories of failure in youth ministry.

We heard comments like . . .

> *I was going to do work today, but I'm just going to read these stories instead.*
>
> *I am laughing so hard my boss just came in to make sure I was okay.*
>
> *I tried to discreetly read these stories during my staff meeting — huge mistake.*
>
> *I'm crying.*
>
> *I will never stop laughing.*

That's when someone finally suggested, "Hey. Can we turn these stories into a book?"

Why, yes. Yes we can.

After a bit of editing (because youth pastors are terrible spellers), we gathered more than two hundred of the stories that were shared with us and put them in this book. Why? Well, for a few reasons.

1. **Because it's funny.** Like, so funny. Just wait until you get to the story about the "resurrection" sermon.
2. **Because we need to laugh at ourselves.** No matter how cool or wise or experienced you are, let's face it: you're also a total idiot sometimes. Whether you contributed a story to this book or not, we're guessing you'll see some of your own ministry fails reflected in these pages. We're hoping this book is a reminder that, as youth workers, we should always take our calling seriously . . . but not ourselves.
3. **Because we need to be reminded we're not alone.** At some point in our ministry careers, we've probably all felt like a little bit of a failure. If you've been there (or you're there right now), we hope this book

makes you laugh, but we also hope it helps you have a little bit more grace for yourself. We've all made mistakes in ministry, and we'll all continue to make mistakes in ministry, but those mistakes don't have to be the end of our stories.

4. **Because the only thing better than learning from *your* mistakes is learning from *someone else's* mistakes.** Think of this book as two-hundred-something pages' worth of ministry coaching, but, like, in reverse. The ideas in this book are terrible. Horrible. Some of the worst. Whatever you read in these following pages, always do the opposite.

And, hey, in case no one has told you this recently: thank you for investing in the lives of teenagers. Even when you accidentally punch them in the face, tell them Santa doesn't exist, or let them get attacked by wild monkeys, you are impacting their lives and their faith in ways you can't even imagine.

You're making a difference and, friend, it's a good one.

One summer, we moved our middle school service to one of our students' backyards. At the time, I was wrapping up a series about trusting God and was planning to do a trust fall during my talk as an object lesson. But when I arrived and surveyed the family's yard, I had an idea that was sure to make this the most epic trust fall in the history of trust falls.

When the time came for me to give my talk, I had my students sit on the cement patio between the family's pool and garage, handed them a bed sheet, and climbed onto the roof of the garage to teach. (Getting nervous yet?) As I reached the pinnacle of my message, I told my students to stand, grab the edges of the bed sheet, and pull it tight. I turned around, ready to perform the world's greatest trust fall, and stepped backward off the roof.

I landed so hard I ripped the bed sheet out of my students' hands and landed flat on my back on the cement. I haven't done a trust fall since.

During a series about dealing with pressure, I decided to do an object lesson by wrapping rubber bands around a watermelon until it exploded. I knew it was going to be messy, so I set up a ton of tarps to catch all the watermelon shrapnel I was expecting.

As I taught, I started adding more and more rubber bands to the watermelon. I kept teaching and the suspense was mounting, but . . . the watermelon was still holding strong. After nearly an hour (and countless rubber bands), the watermelon still refused to explode. Eventually, when my message was long over, I gave up on the object lesson. The watermelon may not have exploded, but I figured we could at least slice it up and make a snack out of it.

I picked up the watermelon, still wrapped in rubber bands, and stepped off the tarps.

And that's when it exploded.

There was a point in my ministry career when we were all really into doing Forrest Gump impressions. It was constant. We quoted that movie all the time. So just before the new school started, I decided to surprise my students with a movie night in our youth room. We made popcorn, pulled a few couches together, turned off the lights, and — you guessed it — cued up *Forrest Gump*.

It had been a while since I'd seen the movie and my memory was a little fuzzy, but it's not like it was rated R or anything. I felt pretty good about it . . . until I remembered there was sex scene.

With only seconds to spare, I jumped out of my seat, sprinted to the back of the room, and quickly turned off the video feed.

But, uh . . . I couldn't figure out how turn off the audio.

KATIE

My church is the oldest church in my city. It has these gorgeous wood floors, high ceilings, and amazing acoustics.

On my last day as an intern, the leadership decided to bring me before the congregation during the adult service to honor me and my time there. It was a pretty big deal.

But as I walked toward the alter, I missed the first step, Jennifer-Lawrence-style. As I fell, I flung out my arm to grab something to steady myself. What I grabbed was a freestanding column, which also fell over, taking out a stack of brass offering plates, which sent every single plate spinning and hitting the wooden floor one . . . by . . . one.

I have never been less excited about those amazing acoustics. I might as well have knocked over an entire drum set.

When I was brand new to student ministry, I saw a game from Stuff You Can Use called Giant Angry Birds, where you launch exercise balls (decorated like Angry Birds) from a gigantic sling shot and try to knock over stacks of cardboard boxes. I loved it, so I decided to try something similar — but on a smaller scale, with water balloon launchers and small bean bags. Then I had an even better idea! Instead of using plain old boring cardboard boxes as targets, I put some of my small group leaders inside the boxes and let them run around as moving targets.

Two things I did not anticipate: first, when fired from a water balloon launcher, bean bags will pierce a cardboard box like a bullet. Second, my students had impeccable aim.

By the end of the game, my poor leaders were literally bruised and bleeding.

One week, I felt like it was important to remind my students that I would never play favorites with them because they were all equally important to me. There was not a single person in that room, I explained, who I loved more than anyone else. No one!

That's when a small voice from the back called out, "Thanks, dad."

I had forgotten my daughter had just moved up into my ministry.

My biggest fail in youth ministry has to be our "Smashing Idols" night, where I thought it would be a good idea to (literally) smash some idols.

During my message, I told my students my Master's degree had become an idol for me so I pulled out a lighter, set it on fire, and threw it into a trash can.

Seconds later, the trash can was on fire. Panicked, I grabbed the paper from the trash can, threw it on the floor, and stomped on it.

I did *not* burn down my church that night, but the carpet was pretty scorched.

At every youth service, I have an adult volunteer who's responsible for collecting the weekly offering and then immediately delivering it to our financial office.

One week, our pastor's wife (who was also our executive administrator), visited our ministry to observe. After the service, she asked, "So, what happens to the offering when your volunteer isn't here — like today?"

I blinked. Suddenly, I realized my offering volunteer hadn't showed up in months. I have no idea where the offering had been going all those weeks, but I'm guessing one of our teenagers was pretty happy about getting a little extra pocket change for a while.

Oops?

BRIAN

I once challenged all of our students to take the Proverbs Challenge — you know, read all 31 chapters of Proverbs in one month, one chapter every day.

I thought it was a great idea. That is, until the mom of one of our newest middle school students came up to me and demanded, "Um, why are you making my seventh grader read about prostitutes?"

Maybe I should've given our middle school families a heads up about that part.

NATALIE

Leading up to a youth group pool party, I spent a lot of time talking to my students about purity and the importance of choosing modest swimsuits.

The night of the pool party, I was so excited to see that no one had dressed inappropriately.

I didn't notice it immediately, but the strap of my swimsuit broke while I was swimming.

And then the front of my swimsuit . . .
slid . . .
slowly . . .
down.

In front of all of my students.

Fail.

CLAIRE

In my first month at my church, I went to a high school guys' small group to teach the lesson. When I got there, they initiated me like they initiate every guy into their small group: I had to drink 1.5 liters of passion fruit flavored soda in one go.

And I did it! Acually, I was the only person to ever complete the challenge without puking.

That is, until I opened my mouth to teach the small group lesson.

I threw up everywhere.

They still talk about it to this day.

RICH

We had a pretty busy weekend recently. We had a student lock-in on Friday night, a funeral on Saturday that I was helping with, and a student baptism on Sunday morning.

After the lock-in and the funeral, I was exhausted, but I still needed to fill the baptistry before Sunday morning. I knew it would take about three hours to fill, so I started the faucet, went home to the parsonage next door, and took a quick nap. Except I missed my three-hour alarm and woke up . . . the next morning.

I sprinted to the church, but it was too late. When I opened the door, it sounded like a waterfall. The choir loft, nursery, and classrooms in the basement were all flooded. On a Sunday morning.

We managed to clean up most of the water before the service started. But my student who was going to get baptized? He never showed up.

JASON

My biggest fail happened during my first month in youth ministry. I was a new dad at the time and, during our youth service, my son needed his diaper changed. When things were up and running, I stepped into a classroom to take care of the diaper change.

Except the room was already occupied.
By two teenagers.
Who were making out.

We all froze, but I was so flustered, all I could think to say was, "Sorry!"

Then I closed the door and left.

STEPHEN

Our worship leader, Dale, was out sick one week, so I decided to fill in for him. I may not be as talented as he is, but I figured I could sing and play guitar well enough to get us by.

By the middle of the worship time, I thought I was doing a pretty good job. That is, until one of our students with special needs yelled over the music, "Boo! Where's Dale?"

He continued yelling until the music was over.

My poor students didn't know how to react, but I thought it was pretty priceless.

When I was an intern, I pulled a prank on a student that got a little out of hand. I added some dye to a bottle of root beer — a dye that would turn, um, certain things (which you would only discover when you went to the bathroom) a bright neon blue.

Unfortunately, the blue dye was too obvious once it had been added to the root beer, so I needed to find a way to get the student to drink the root beer in the dark, where he couldn't see the blue dye. Where could I find somewhere dark? The movie theater, of course!

I picked up my student, took him to the movies, and bought tickets to whatever movie was about to start. The movie didn't matter to me, so long as that kid drank the root beer!

Well, turns out the movie that was about to start was pretty inappropriate. I don't even know if the prank worked because I was so busy apologizing to parents that I completely forgot to ask about it.

In my second week as a first time ministry director, I was determined to make a big splash. A movement called The Ice Bucket Challenge had just gone viral through social media, so I thought I could take that idea and use it with my students.

I called my version Ice For Christ. I filmed a video of myself getting drenched in ice water, challenged my students do the same, and then prepared myself for a huge, gigantic, monumental, viral response!

Except no one participated.

But I guess I still made a splash?

AARON

One week, I let our high school students lead our entire middle school service. We met beforehand to talk about what they had planned and it sounded great. One of our senior guys would be speaking about the death and resurrection of Jesus and I was pumped!

That is, until he said Jesus was a zombie.

Our middle schoolers were very confused.

JUAN

To honor one of our high school graduates, I went to a local Christian bookstore and picked up a really nice navy gift Bible for him. It was pretty awesome. I even had it engraved with his name.

Unfortunately, I'm colorblind. So, apparently, I actually gave him a purple Bible covered in flowers.

GREG

We once put on a huge event for high schoolers where we set up a bunch of activities throughout our building so they could keep themselves entertained before the program. One of those activities was an amazing obstacle course we built. You had to run up some stairs, dive through a tunnel, then grab a rope and swing down to the floor.

Once we set it up, we thought it might be fun to have students swing from the platform into a kiddie pool. We didn't really have anything to fill the kiddie pool with, except about a dozen balloons, so we blew them up and tossed them into the pool as a pop of color.

Unfortunately, when students looked down at the pool from the platform and saw the layer of balloons, they thought the balloons would provide a soft landing, so they flung their bodies into that thing with no reservations. The first kid jumped butt-first, popped one balloon, scattered the others, and landed directly on the cement floor on his tail bone.

SETH

I was running short on time one week, but I still needed an image for the screen during that week's game. Desperate, I grabbed a funny picture of a cartoon frog from Google Images and used it to make a quick graphic. (And yeah, I know that's technically stealing. Don't do it.)

Well, thank goodness for tech teams, because right before the service started, the guy running slides that morning said, "Hey dude, you sure you want to use that frog picture? You can see its wiener."

I don't make last-minute graphics anymore.

We take our students to a summer camp every year that splits students into teams and then has them compete in a variety of competitions throughout the week. One year, they added a new competition where every team had to build a team mascot using only materials they already had at camp.

We were on the black team, so we thought it would be funny to create a black sheep as our mascot. We found some cardboard boxes, duct tape, black sharpies, glue, and sent our students off to build something.

When our student debuted their black sheep a few hours later, I thought it was pretty good. It even seemed to have some kind of woolly texture. "Guys," I asked them, "what is this?"

That's when my high school guys showed me their legs. They had all shaved their bodies and glued their own hair to the sheep mascot.

The whole thing smelled like a hamster cage.

SUZETTE

I'll admit it: I'm a little competitive. It's possible that I've embarrassed my small group once or twice, like the time we were competing in a giant city-wide scavenger hunt with the other high school small groups.

When we reached one of our stops on the scavenger hunt, I realized a guys' groups was catching up to us and I was not about to let that happen. I dove back into my SUV and screamed at my group of tenth graders to hurry up and get back in the car.

As soon as I heard a door slam, I backed up, ready to fly out of the parking lot, when I felt my SUV hit a small bump. The girls in the backseat all screamed. One of my girls was still in the parking lot . . . and I had just run over her foot.

The good news: after they released her from the hospital, she came back and finished the race with us. The bad news: we didn't win.

We had big plans for a glow-in-the-dark-themed outreach night. We invited tons of middle schoolers and planned a tons of glow-in-the-dark games and activities. We were going to do glow-in-the-dark face paint, glow sticks, glow bracelets, and big group games with glowing volleyballs, soccer balls, and more.

The event was a huge hit in terms of attendance . . . but our big glow-in-the-dark activities were a total flop. None of the balls for the outdoor games would light up, no mater how hard we tried. We tried to recover by quickly spraying them with glow-in-the-dark spray paint, by wrapping them in glow sticks, and even by outlining the fields in glow sticks. It all failed. You couldn't see a thing.

Fortunately, our middle schoolers were happy simply hanging out with each other, even without the cool games.

I once planned an entire event themed around big, crazy, messy games. We planned a game called Fast Food Bowling, where we poured ketchup and mustard on the ground and made students slide through it on their bellies as they tried to knock over french-fry-shaped bowling pins. We did another one that involved students dressed like babies, pouring gallons of milk into pitchers as they waded through kiddie pools filled with packing peanuts. And we had another game where students would snowboard on the Wii Fit, while we created a "blizzard" with giant fans, spray bottles filled with water, and bags of flour.

I knew it was going to be messy, so I was prepared . . . but not prepared enough.

I covered the entire floor of our student space in tarps and duct taped them down to protect the carpet. Unfortunately, the packing peanuts soaked up the ketchup, mustard, and milk, then lodged themselves in the tread of students' shoes like tiny disgusting sponges and left footprints everywhere they went — even outside of the tarped areas. At the end of the night, when I pulled back the tarped areas, you could see the tarp had clearly worked. Where it had been taped, the carpet was perfectly clean. Everywhere else was sticky and black.

Oh and you know that flour blizzard? I had no idea just how far airborne flour could travel. It covered every surface in the room: the entire cafe, the door handles, the stage, the sound equipment, and the entire tech booth.

When that event was over, we used every vacuum cleaner, mop, sponge, and bottle of multipurpose cleaner we could find in the building. The even ended at 9:00pm, but I think I went home at 3:00am.

One night we played a game where I gave my students a choice between a box containing a mystery object or cold hard cash. We gave away a bunch of weird items and a little cash, but for the final contestant we decided to go all out. We chose a high school guy who was visiting for the first time and told him he could choose between a mystery box or $200. Yeah — two hundred dollars.

Since I knew there was no way that high schooler was going to turn down $200 in cash, I didn't think it really mattered what I put in the box. So I put my car keys inside.

Well, he chose the box.

Before I could say I hadn't really meant to give away my own car, the crowd had already hoisted the kid into the air in celebration. Everyone went nuts.

In that kind of situation, there is no graceful way to regain control.

My biggest fail was actually one of my students' biggest fails, but I guess being a youth pastor means you have to anticipate moments like this one. I had taken a group of high schoolers to the beach to enjoy a little fun in the sun. Everyone was jumping into the ocean from a pier and things seemed to be going well . . . until the kid with a broken back decided to jump. Into the ocean. And he couldn't swim.

Don't worry, we fished him out.

At some point in your youth ministry career, you realize that teenagers can injure themselves doing just about anything. For me, it was during a thumb war tournament.

Pro tip: don't let eighth graders battle sixth graders (especially first-time visitors) in a thumb war, unless you're prepared for nearly dislocated thumbs, a whole lot of tears, and uncomfortable conversations with parents.

JEFF

It was our fall kick-off campfire night and I was looking for a cheap and easy dinner for my students. While I was shopping, I found a box of hot dogs for an unbelievable price, so I grabbed them for our dinner.

It turns out those "hot dogs" were actually raw breakfast sausages.

Did you know it takes 30 minutes to cook one of those things over a campfire?

DANIELLE

We played a late-night game of Grog in the church one night. If you're not familiar with the game, it involves a lot of running and hiding in the dark.

Unsurprisingly, one of our students took a spill. Unfortunately, it was down a flight of stairs. She complained her foot was hurting, but I was pretty sure she was just being a baby so I gave her an ice pack and told her she'd be fine.

The next day, she went to the hospital. As it turns out, it was a pretty nasty break and she was in a cast for six weeks. Oops.

STEVEN

To celebrate Cinco de Mayo, we threw an event with games, piñatas, and tacos — but like, all at the same time. We filled piñatas with taco meat, salsa, lettuce, and cheese and made a game out of it. Students had to break open the piñatas and then race to assemble and eat a taco from the ingredients.

We knew it was going to be messy, but for some reason the piñatas were partially filled with candy in addition to the taco fillings. When those piñatas burst open and ground-beef-covered candies started flying all over the room, everyone went nuts. Everywhere there were students digging through salsa, dodging the kids who were still swinging bats, and downing candy covered in cheese.

It was pretty gross, but those students still ask if we can do it again.

My biggest youth ministry fail? Oh, just last night! I moved a chair for a game just as a parent was sitting on it. Didn't even see her. Good times.

ROBBY

During prayer time, one of my students asked us to pray that she would find a way to get the community service hours she needed to qualify for the National Honor Society. Confused, I asked about the many hours she had volunteered at our church. She said her teacher had decided not to give her credit for those hours. Jokingly, I said, "Well maybe we should pray for your teacher's surgery to have that stick removed."

I guess my student didn't get the joke because the next time I saw that teacher, she thanked me for the prayers.

Not my proudest moment.

We were hosting a session of our camp in an off-site location that didn't belong to us. At the end of the session, our speaker challenged one of our young staffers (who had a parkour habit) to do a wall flip.

Our students were so excited to see what they were sure was going to be an epic flip.

The kid ran toward the wall, leaped, planted one foot on the wall, and then — *BOOM*.

His feet went through the wall.

Lesson learned: don't let anyone do parkour on drywall unless you're prepared to pay for the damages.

AARON

I know it's usually our students who are getting injured at youth events, but at our last Nerf War event, it was me.

My intention was to run up a flight of stairs and then drop into a cool Rambo-style rolling dive. My reality looked more like me tripping on a stair, smashing into a wall, and breaking my wrist.

JOHNATHAN

We were playing a game called Hoodie Legs, where students put their arms and legs into the sleeves of a gigantic hoodie and then have to perform a series of tasks. One of our tasks involved getting on a scooter. The game is hilarious to watch, but having your arms and legs stuffed inside a hoodie definitely makes it difficult to break a fall . . . so the scooter was maybe not the best idea.

One of our guys (the one you'd expect) got a little carried away, ignored our safety precautions, fell off the scooter face-first on the gym floor, and broke his front tooth in half.

I felt terrible.

But I also kind of wanted to tell him to follow the rules next time.

JOHN

So you know how pasta dinner fund raisers are popular because pasta is so easy to make? Well you haven't met me or my students.

We were hosting a pasta dinner for about a hundred people as a way to raise funds for our mission trip. Before the event, we put the water on to boil and turned on a movie to help pass the time. An hour later, we realized we never put the pasta in the water.

At that point, the event was about to begin and we were scrambling. We boiled a fresh pot of water and heated up the cream sauce in a second pot. No one thought to stir the noodles after they were dropped into the water, so they turned into a brick of pasta goop. No one thought to stir the cream sauce either, which burned. The only thing that wasn't ruined was the garlic bread, but that's because no one ever turned on the oven.

COOPER

In my second year as an intern, we had a huge turnout for our big summer kick-off event. I felt great about it. To start the program, I was hosting a game where we filled the inside of a pool noodle with milk, positioned a student on either end of the noodle, and made them blow into it as hard as they could. The loser would end up with milk all over them. It's a fun, silly, and gross game that I thought we were ready for.

You know what we were not ready for? The stubborn determination of a junior high boy. That kid blew into that noodle so hard he blacked out. Seriously. It was like I was watching everything in slow motion. I watched him black out, tumble backward, fall off the stage, and hit his head against some concrete steps.

He ended up being fine (and I ended up keeping my job), but we will never play that game again.

TRACY

If you thought Cooper's story was a once-in-a-lifetime occurrence, hang on. The exact same thing happened to us during that pool noodle game. Two brothers went head-to-head and the older brother passed out. We played with a raw egg instead of milk, so he ended up unconscious *and* with egg all over his face. Oops.

THOMAS

For my very first lock-in, I was in charge of running the inflatable sumo wrestling game — you know, the one where two students dress up in giant inflatable sumo suits and try to wrestle.

The night had just begun and one of my first match-ups was a teenage couple. Within seconds, the teenage boy thought it would be funny to run full-speed at his girlfriend, who weighed maybe 100 pounds. When they made contact, she flew fifteen feet across the room and slammed her head against the floor.

The police, paramedics, and the girl's parents all showed up. She was fine, but it's been six years and I still get reminded of this incident on a regular basis.

KENNY

Since we're on the subject of kids flying across the room and slamming their heads on the floor, let me tell you about one of my fail stories.

If you watch *Ellen*, you might be familiar with her game, Aw Snap! In it, two contestants stand back-to-back and are connected with a bungee cord. When the game begins, the contestants run in opposite directions, trying to be the first to grab and eat an apple that's waiting for them on their side of the room without being snapped backward by their opponent.

The game was hilarious with adults, so I figured it would be just as funny with kids — and it might even be safer, since they wouldn't be strong enough to really snap each other very hard. Well, my instincts were wrong. Middle schoolers may not be as strong as adults, but they weigh a lot less . . . which means they fly a lot farther. So maybe don't try this one with preteens.

JACOB

Once, I decided to set aside an entire month as "Gross Game Month." For a whole month, I thought, we would only play gross games. To kick things off, we played a game where five students each had to eat one gross food: dry oatmeal, an entire box of Whoppers, Vienna sausages, a raw onion, and gefilte fish.

After the first bite, Gefilte Fish Kid threw up.
Raw Onion Kid threw up second.
Vienna Sausage Girl threw up third.

And then fourteen more kids in the audience threw up just from watching the scene unfold.

Seventeen students puked that night. Do you think that's maybe a world record?

NICKOLAS

One week, I was using my fingers to count out a few points before dismissing my students to small groups. When I got to number one, they all started laughing.

I looked down. I had accidentally been using my middle finger.

TRAVIS

A few years ago, we had just started a new youth ministry at a church plant, so we only had four students regularly attending. One night, my wife and I were driving a few of them home when a yelling match broke out in the parking lot over who was going to sit in the middle seat. It was dark and everyone was still yelling, but I was pretty sure I had just heard all the doors slam, so I started driving away.

The yelling continued, but this time the yelling was because one of the girls was still only halfway in the moving vehicle. As I drove away, she somehow managed to dive into the car and shut the door behind her.

I almost killed 25% of my youth group that day.

JAI

On the first day of our summer conference one year, a junior high girl was really excited to show me her new Bible. Of course, I was excited with her, but when she opened its pages I was not prepared for the size of the font. It was huge!

Taken aback, I joked, "Holy smokes, that writing is huge! What, are you going blind?"

Uh . . . turns out she actually *was* going blind. I've never felt so awful.

Once, we played Sardines in the church.
The *entire* church.
Even the sanctuary.
The sanctuary with the pipe organ.

Did you know twelve teenagers can fit inside a pipe organ?

Did you also know twelve teenagers in a pipe organ will cause about $6,000 in damages?

Well now you do.

ROGER

When I first started in student ministry, I wanted to plan an incredible New Year's Eve party. It was going to be 70's-themed. I delegated games and decor to volunteers. I even hired a band from two hours away. It was going to be awesome . . . I thought.

No one showed up.

Literally.

No one.

Let's just say I learned a lot about event promotion and communication that day.

SAMANTHA

One week, we did an icebreaker contest to see who (if anyone) could stand to eat three progressively hotter peppers. For some reason, one boy thought this was either a joke, a race, or both, because he shoveled all three peppers into his mouth as fast as he could.

He spent the rest of the night alternating between drinking lots of milk and disappearing to the bathroom for a while.

So just a reminder: teenagers have no common sense, so make your game instructions *really* clear.

I once took a group of students to a ranch to ride horses. Unfortunately, when we arrived, a few kids turned out to be pretty afraid of the horses. To put their minds at ease, I told them how friendly the horses were, how safe it was to ride them, and how fun the day would be.

Eventually, I got every student on a horse and we were on our way with the help of a guide. A few minutes into the ride, one of the horses got turned around. Our guide walked over to get the horse back on track, but when she approached, the horse kicked her. In the chest. Three times. While all of my students watched in horror.

The guide was fine, but the horse carrying my most skiddish student got spooked and bolted back toward the barn with my student screaming the entire the way. Later, another horse walked into a beehive and the student it was carrying was stung more than twenty times. So yeah, it was a pretty successful trip.

TYLER

A youth pastor friend of mine (who shall not be named) was taking a huge group of high schoolers to summer camp for a week. The travel timing was super tight because of the number of students attending, so it was important to stick to their schedule.

Thirty minutes into the trip, a high schooler asked to make a bathroom stop. My friend told him he could either use the bathroom on the back of the bus or wait a couple of hours for their first scheduled bathroom stop. He went back to his seat.

Fifteen minutes later, he asked again. He didn't want to use the bathroom on the bus, he said, because he had to poop. This time, he was panicked, but he again agreed to return to his seat.

Fifteen minutes after that, the kid screamed, "THIS BUS HAS TO STOP RIGHT NOW."

Seeing the panic in his eyes, my friend agreed

to stop the bus. As they pulled into a Cracker Barrel parking lot, the kid jumped out of the bus and sprinted to the bathroom with my friend chasing behind him.

The student ran into the bathroom, grabbed a stall door, and gave it a furious tug. It was locked. Unfortunately for that student (and my friend), things had already been set in motion.

When my friend caught up to the student, he heard two things: his student muttering, "Oh no, oh no, oh no, oh no," and a Cracker Barrel customer shouting, "Oh snap! That dude just ____ his pants!" And it wasn't just his pants. By the time my friend arrived, it had fallen out of the student's pants and onto the floor.

A few minutes later, the student silently returned to his seat on the bus, wearing a pair of ill-fitting pleated shorts he borrowed from a volunteer.

Not a single word was said.

My biggest youth ministry fails have been run-ins with the police.

The first time, I thought it would be a good idea to paint a sign in the church parking lot at 10:00pm. That almost got me arrested for vandalism.

The second time, again late at night, I found myself chasing two students across the church lawn with a water gun when a cop pulled up and yelled at me to freeze.

I can laugh about those moments now but, at the time . . . not so much.

Once, I shot a student with a BB gun.
It was an accident.
I promise.

But the kid I shot is a youth pastor now, so I guess I did something right.

During a parent meeting at my last church, a parent demanded to know why I chose to play a game involving diapers and melted candy bars.

My response? "Well, maybe if your kids didn't always have sticks up their butts, they could relax and enjoy themselves a little bit."

I never did figure out why I didn't last very long at that church.

ERIC

A few years ago, I was a high school camp director for the summer. One day, we planned an off-site activity where we would drive our high schoolers 40 minutes to the base of a mountain, set out on a hike, eat dinner together, have an evening service, and come back. Pretty simple, right? Yeah, no.

We were 35 minutes into our 40 minute drive when we realized a girl was missing. We'd left her behind. Only five minutes away from our destination, we turned around to go retrieve her. When we arrived, we learned that she was diabetic and had missed the bus because she had passed out from low blood sugar. After we left without her, she woke up alone and panicked. Awesome. We got some sugar in her, made sure she was good to go, and then hopped back on the bus.

40 minutes later, with our van rides finally complete, we were ready for the hike. We hiked up the mountain in a few small groups. Everyone made it to the top — even the girl

who had passed out a few hours earlier! I felt great. It seemed like the day was turning around. Boy was I wrong.

We hiked back down the mountain, loaded up our vans, and drove to the home where we were going to have dinner and our evening service. When we arrived, we learned two boys were missing. They had gotten lost on their way back down the mountain — and one of them was diabetic! This wasn't even a diabetes camp! What's up with that?

A few of us drove back to the mountain and searched for hours with no sign of them. Just as I was about to call the missing boys' parents, a truck pulled up. The boys jumped out. Somehow they had made it down the mountain, found their way to a highway, got some sugar for the guy with diabetes, and hitchhiked (yeah — *hitchhiked*) to the home where we were having dinner.

In the end, everyone was fine, but *wow* did I feel like a failure. I guess you could say we learned a lot about what (not) to do when you're planning an off-site activity. That's good, right?

ANDY

We once had the brilliant idea of doing a Happy Meal Eating Contest right before worship. Sounds harmless, right? Well, the twist was that we put the entire thing in a blender and contestants had to drink it. That's a cheeseburger, an order of fries, and an orange soda all blended together.

Two student volunteers only took two small sips before they both needed a garbage can. The entire room cleared out.

That wasn't exactly the smoothest transition into worship that we've ever done.

BRIAN

After a "destruction of property" instance on a Wednesday night, we were instructed to keep our students restricted to the youth space for a while. The following week, a group of girls asked me if they could stop by the main sanctuary for a few minutes to look for a lost item. I gave them permission but told them to be back in five minutes.

When they didn't return, I left to track them down. Once I found them, I went off. One girl tried to interrupt me, but I wasn't having it. They'd broken my trust and I was not happy.

As they walked back to the youth space, I took a moment to collect my thoughts. That's when I saw a woman who looked like she had been crying. When I asked her what was wrong, she told me she had been praying for a sign that there were still people who cared for her, when a group of teenage girls had walked by, welcomed her, and prayed with her.

Yeah. Sorry, girls.

TONY

Buckle up. This story's a long one.

I was the new youth pastor at one of my previous churches and had only been there for a short time when a group of students told me I was going to take them to Cedar Point. "It's a tradition," they said.

Being young, new, and eager to please, I made it happen. More than forty kids signed up, so I organized a caravan of ten vehicles to transport everyone. I figured it would take about five hours to get there, so I planned to leave at 5:00am, get there around 10:00am, spend the day at the park, and be back the church by 2:00am.

Shortly after 5:00am, we were off! Until, just a few minutes later, we got our first request for a bathroom break. At first I told them to hold it, but when they told me it was "a girl thing," I hurried up and pulled over. Of course, before I could put a stop to it, all forty students got out of the vehicles. Not all at once though.

Every minute or two, another student or two would get out and head to the bathroom. Thirty minutes later, we were finally back on the road.

Two hours into the drive, a blinding rainstorm rolled in. It was so bad, I decided to pull over and signaled to the rest of the caravan to pull over as well. Looking back, I noticed a vehicle full of girls was missing. Back then, cell phones weren't really a thing, so we waited, assuming they'd catch up soon. They didn't.

After the rain let up, I let a few of the vehicles head toward the theme park while I sent a scout car back down the highway to look for the missing girls' vehicle. Ten minutes after the scout car left, the girls reappeared . . . with no scout car in sight.

A few minutes later, we saw what we thought was the scout car fly by us on the highway, so we pulled back onto the road and tried to catch up with them. They were going fast though and catching up with them wasn't easy. It wasn't until we arrived at Cedar Point that we caught up with them . . . only to discover it hadn't been them at all. The scout car was still missing.

By the time I arrived at the park, everyone else (besides the scout car) had already been there for some time. They were laying in the parking lot, waiting, because — oh yeah — I had everyone's tickets.

Everyone headed into the park while I waited outside for the scout car to arrive. Two hours later, they still hadn't arrived, so I went inside to meet the rest of the group for lunch.

About five minutes after I went inside, the scout car arrived and, having no way to contact me, bought their own tickets and headed into the park. When they found us, I realized I had $200 worth of nonrefundable tickets still in my pocket, so I went into the parking lot to see if I could sell them . . . until I was stopped by park security and threatened with ejection if I didn't stop scalping tickets on their property.

We planned to leave at 10:00pm. Of course, we didn't leave until 11:00pm.

When we finally got to the parking lot, we discovered one of the vehicles had a flat tire, which took thirty minutes to change. The spare tire, though, came with a warning not to exceed 55 mph — at least 15 mph slower than I was anticipating.

I made the decision to let eight of the ten cars go ahead at normal speed while I crept along with the slow car. Ten cars, two groups. It was supposed to be simple. Stick with your group. Easy! Yeah, right.

One car in the first group tried to take a short cut and got lost. My wife, one of the drivers, was so tired that another adult in the vehicle had to help her stay alert. Just a few minutes from the church, another car hit a cow — yeah, a cow.

We were supposed to arrive back at the church at 2:00am. My car pulled into the church parking lot at around 5:30am.

I could write another ten pages about the messages I received, the phone calls I had to return, and the tough lessons I learned from that trip, but I'll let you use your imagination.

During a youth lock-in, we turned the church into a massive Capture the Flag Dodgeball game. The game was moving, but we were ready to transition to our next segment. To end on a high note, I decided to call a free-for-all. "Two minutes left, no outs!"

You'd be surprised how much chaos can happen in two minutes. Both teams converged in the foyer, dodgeballs were flying, people were screaming — and that's when my senior pastor showed up.

Nothing like accidentally turning your lock-in into a massive riot.

ROB

We once held a back-to-school rally with about forty students at a regional park. We had scoured the town for tons of cardboard boxes and planned to let our students turn those boxes into a gigantic maze.

To help them assemble the maze, we brought lots of duct tape and plenty of utility knives.

Once the maze was complete, we started gathering up all the unused boxes, duct tape, and utility knives.

A few feet from me, there was a small cardboard box that seemed like a good place to collect all of our tools. I had a utility knife in my hand, so I tossed it into the box.

Well . . . the box wasn't empty. There was a sixth grade girl inside. A sixth grade girl who then needed stitches for the minor stab wound in her back.

I once asked my church for suggestions for a service project that my students could do. Their idea? Paint the kitchen.

Maybe I was a little naive, but I thought this was a great idea. It took five weeks of work, three times the paint it should have required, and countless hours of me and my volunteers re-painting the places where my students had messed up.

But, hey, that kitchen looked pretty good . . . eventually.

STEVEN

In my first summer of youth ministry, I did a 4th of July event involving sparklers and fireworks. The problem? I realized too late that we didn't have enough lighters to do both at the same time. As my adults were lighting fireworks, kids were hovering over them trying to light their sparklers from the same flame. Not the safest thing I've ever done.

Plus, we lit a few smoke bombs, which turned out to be way smokier than I anticipated. The smoke actually filled our entire church building, right in the middle of a business meeting.

Literally everyone with the power to fire me was sitting in a room that was filling with smoke, thanks to my stupid fireworks idea.

STEPHANIE

We were on a field trip across state with a bus, four vans, and 134 people. On the way home, we stopped at a rest station. When everyone got back on the bus, we did a head count, but one of my volunteers and I couldn't agree on our count. I felt like we were missing someone.

We asked the bus driver, but he said we had everyone, and pulled away.

Twenty miles later, I screamed, *Home-Alone*-style, "Has anyone seen Carson?"

It turns out that I am, in fact, an excellent head-counter . . . because we definitely left Carson alone at a gas station for a while.

When I was in high school, one of my youth pastor's ministry fails was legendary. He had taken our group on a mission trip from Kansas to Mexico and traveled by van. On the way home, they drove through the night with our youth pastor at the wheel. Everyone else was fast asleep.

At some point, he turned onto the wrong interstate. With no one awake to correct him, he kept going. Six hours later, he realized he was in Colorado. Not Kansas.

We used to do a monthly evening service where we served communion using small glasses. After those services, it was usually my responsibility to make sure those glasses got washed.

One month, a number of high schoolers were lingering after the service while I was cleaning up. With so many tiny communion glasses still full, we did the obvious thing — communion shots.

Not my proudest moment, people.

CARTER

During a retreat, one of our students had a band competition he couldn't miss, so he arranged to have his mom and grandma drop him off the following day.

When the three of them arrived, they parked in the parking lot near the edge of the field where we were playing ultimate frisbee. The student jumped out and joined the game. His mom and grandma got out of the car (cane in hand) and came to chat with me. While we talked, I kept my back to the game of ultimate frisbee happening on the field behind me. That's why I never saw this coming.

In the middle of our conversation, the student who had just arrived sprinted down the field after the frisbee. He was so focused on the frisbee, he didn't realize where he was running. That kid hit his grandma so hard, they both went flying. Everyone was fine, but I will never forget the visual of that kid body slamming his own grandma into the ground.

CHAD

At camp one year, a boy was goofing around on a top bunk, fell, and dislocated his shoulder at 1:00am. I was not expecting to spend my night driving twenty miles to the nearest ER, but after a few hours of medication and treatment and a quick stop at a local gas station to fill up on sugar and fried burritos, we were heading back to camp. I know I shouldn't laugh, but he was so doped up on pain pills that I couldn't help myself. If I hadn't been driving, I could've gotten a pretty hilarious video out of that car ride.

SARAH

Once, a few middle schoolers asked if they could make popcorn. Microwave popcorn seemed to me like a fairly fool-proof activity, so I told them to go ahead.

Fifteen minutes later, I realized I was wrong. They had taken a bag of microwave popcorn, emptied its contents into a mini carnival-style popcorn popper, which they had found somewhere in the church, and walked away.

When I found it, it was smoking profusely. I unplugged it, grabbed it by its top, and held it out the nearest window. Well, the top was not attached to the rest of the machine, so the entire thing fell out the window and into the church garden two stories below.

I inherited a youth ministry a few years ago. But, somehow, no one told me what the ministry was actually called until after I got there. I think the name was inspired by the Bible verse, "No one can snatch them from the Father's hand" (John 10:29 NLT).

Let's just say there is one word in that verse that should absolutely never be used as the name of a youth ministry.

ERIC

We once hosted a Valentine's Day fund raiser to help send students to camp. We planned to serve a full meal, which meant we had to prep food the night before and the day of the event.

The problems started almost immediately. We were halfway through mixing the ingredients for our red velvet cookies when we broke the standing mixer, which was on loan from our pastor's wife. It literally started smoking. Our pastor kindly brought us a replacement, but we almost immediately broke that one too.

The next morning, we were working on the spaghetti and sauce when I had to step out for a few minutes. It was just spaghetti — what could go wrong? Well, when I came back, the spaghetti was scorched and stuck together in a clump. Also, we made the cookies way too big and didn't have enough for everyone.

I think we'll do things a little differently next time.

DANIEL

When I was a camp counselor, we all had to do trust falls. I hate those things (maybe I'm not very trusting), but I gave it a shot. When I fell backward, one of the guys supposed to be catching me stood with arms folded across his chest. I hit him so hard and in such a way that his arms dug into his chest and broke a couple of ribs.

JAMES

One of my seniors in high school thought it would be funny to attack me from behind with some kind of wrestling move. Well, as soon as I felt something touch my neck, my instincts kicked in. I grabbed the kid's arm, threw him over my shoulder, and pinned him to the ground with my knee on his back.

When I looked up, the room had gone silent and everyone (including my boss) was staring at me.

TALBOT

We once played a game where a couple of kids had to call their grandparents and ask them to define a current slang term. We put the phone calls on speaker so everyone could hear, but when one kid asked his grandma to define "on fleek," she cussed. In front of everyone. My boss didn't think it was quite as funny as I did.

DANIEL

When I was in Bible college as a youth ministry major, I was in charge of creating a youth activity that 50-60 local teenagers would attend. As a college student, this was a big deal for me!

The activity I designed was a real-life version of the board game Clue. We had the characters, weapons, special rooms — everything. It was awesome. I spent three weeks working on that activity and figured it would take two or three hours to solve the crime.

The day game, tons of teenagers showed up, and I was ready for them to try and solve the puzzle.

And they did.
In fifteen minutes.

We still had almost three hours to go! Talk about making things up on the spot. I don't know how those kids solved it so fast, but they must've watched too much *CSI*.

RANDY

When I was a young single guy, I planned a mission trip for my students that for some reason involved our team staying in a women's dorm at a Christian college.

On our last day, all the girls from the dorms popped out of their rooms and lined the hallways to say goodbye as we headed to the buses. To my dismay, I suddenly realized I needed to use the bathroom. As our students said their goodbyes, I ran to the bathroom.

Well, I clogged the toilet.
And there was no plunger in sight.

I then made the mistake of asking someone for a plunger, who asked another person, who asked another person. Eventually, the entire building full of college girls knew I had clogged the toilet. Once I had located a plunger, they all watched me carry it to its destination.

To this day, my toes still curl in embarrassment just thinking about it.

MICHAEL

I was recently chatting with my summer interns, a teenage guy and a teenage girl, about ants. For some reason, they were wondering how humans compared to an ant in strength and size.

That's when I butted in to say to our female intern, "I'm pretty sure you're at least 100 times bigger than an ant."

She looked at me. "Is that a fat joke?"

NICK

For our annual Christmas party, we started the night in a different room than we normally do, moving later into the worship center. When it was time to move into the worship center, I realized the lights in there were still turned off.

I ran ahead of my students so I could flip the lights on, but the light switch was on the opposite end of the room. I ran, in the dark, and — *WHAM!* I slammed my face into the corner of a door.

No students saw it happen, so I thought I was in the clear . . . that is, until I got up to start introducing our first game and all my students looked at me in horror. There was blood trickling down the corner of my eye and my face was pretty badly bruised. So embarrassing.

JASON

For my first summer as student pastor, we spent a week at a popular camping area and swimming hole in our area. The swimming hole had a waterfall, a creek, and a rope swing, so my students, of course, were begging to go there.

One afternoon, I gave them the go-ahead and we all headed toward the waterfall as a group. A number of my students ran ahead of the rest of the group — still in my line of sight, but a number of yards ahead of me.

As we got closer to the waterfall, I noticed something I wasn't expecting to see: topless women. I panicked. I quickly yelled for the students at the front of the group to turn around, but it was too late. Some of our high school guys had already seen what I had seen, but fortunately they turned around and helped direct the middle school guys away from the water.

I was mortified.

MATTHEW

Once in a while, I get a little tongue-tied. Most recently, it happened when I was explaining how to play a game involving balloons. I was trying to say, "You can only use two breaths to blow up your balloon. Just two breaths."

Instead, I said "breasts."

I now prefer the term "exhales."

ANDREW

One week before our biggest event of the year, I organized a spontaneous day of summer ice blocking. It's like sledding with a block of ice, instead of snow and a sled. It's pretty fun and I've done it plenty of times.

This time, though, I slipped. I landed on my wrist and heard a crack, but didn't think much of it. On Monday, I went in to get it checked out and learned I had a clean fracture of my arm.

The timing was pretty inconvenient. I had to show up to our biggest event of the year in a huge cast.

NOLAN

I've always been told I have a pretty generic appearance. My entire life, I've been mistaken for other people, but the worst one happened when I was a high-school-aged volunteer in our youth ministry and happened to look a little bit like my youth pastor.

It happened right before a volunteer party. The lights were dim and everyone was mingling, when I felt someone come up behind me, grab my butt, and whisper in my ear.

I spun around. It was my youth pastor's wife and I'm not sure which of us was more horrified.

I know this is weird, but stick with me. When my kids were little, the only way I could get them to wear a coat when it was cold outside was by telling them, "If *you* don't wear your coat, *I'll* get cold." It doesn't make sense, I know, but it worked. As my kids gold older, it turned into a family joke.

When my son was thirteen and on a mission trip with me, he showed up for our work project, on a very hot day, wearing pants instead of shorts. Maybe it was the long day of sweating and hard work that made me forget my filter, but at some point that day I found myself yelling down a hallway, "Take off your pants, you're making me hot!"

At least I didn't follow it up with, "It's okay, he's my son."

BRANDON

I took a huge group of students to Six Flags on the hottest and most crowded day of the summer. It was so hot that people all over the park were throwing up on rides and passing out from heat exhaustion. Rides were closing down left and right. The heat was unbelievable.

The bright spot in the day, though, was that a church member offered to cook us dinner at their home that night. Excited to escape the heat of the day, we piled into the bus at dinner time and drove to their home.

When we got there, we discovered their power had gone out, which meant they had no air conditioning. They had set up a few fans, but those fans were no match for forty sweaty teenagers on the hottest day of the summer.

Oh, and do you want to know what we had for dinner on the hottest night of the summer? Hot biscuits, gravy, and milk.

MACKENZIE

One week we knew we were going to be short on volunteers for our evening service, but we didn't want to cancel. Instead, we decided to have a nice, simple, relaxing movie night. Easy, right?

Well, the students apparently noticed the lack of adults in the room because they went wild. They threw popcorn, tipped couches, and ran wild around the building.

Next time we're that short on volunteers, I think we'll just cancel.

MATT

The first time I took a group of students to camp, I was in charge of a large group game of guys against girls.

After I explained the game, I sent the guys to one side and the girls to another side. One kid though, did not seem to be in the right place.

"Buddy," I said, "you're a guy, so come to the guys' side."

Turns out the kid was, in fact, a girl. And I made her cry on the first day of camp.

CHRIS

We planned for around 50 students at our last lock-in, but more than 100 showed up! It's a good problem to have, but it definitely was a problem. We didn't have enough adult volunteers for all those students, the games we planned couldn't accommodate everyone, and there were times the night became total chaos. We even caught a couple in a closet in various states of undress and had another kid leave the event entirely and walk home.

Like I said, that was our last lock-in.

My students absolutely love to play a game called Aliens. It's a great game to play at night if you have a decent amount of building space with access to two floors.

My students love this game so much that one night I decided to theme our entire program around the concept of aliens. We started out with a great Bible study on how we were "aliens" in the world, and then broke off to play Aliens.

In the very first round, one of our girls was heading to the second floor when she walked on an area of unfinished flooring above the sanctuary. In the dark, she missed the decking and fell through the ceiling into the sanctuary.

Luckily, no bones were broken, but our maintenance guy was really not happy with me.

MICAH

I had only been a youth pastor for a few weeks when I took a group of students to camp. I was still learning all of my students' names.

One night, I was telling my students a story about something that smelled terrible, so I said, "It smelled like B.O.!" I meant "body odor," of course, but just then a student walked in who hadn't showered all week.

His name was Bo.

I haven't used that phrase since.

JOSHUA

The day before I was taking a group of students to a trampoline park, 25 new students unexpectedly signed up to go. That's a pretty big jump in registration and I didn't have enough time to assign all of those new students to vehicles. I knew we would have enough seats to transport them all, but I didn't have time to figure out who would be riding in which vehicles.

Everyone got to the event just fine, but all of the new registrations had really thrown off my ability to track pick-ups when the event was over.

Long story short, we, um, left a kid behind.

SHEENA

For some reason, I thought it would be a good idea to play capture the flag in our sanctuary, in the dark. You can probably guess where this story is going.

Two kids collided at full-speed. Then, as one of those kids was standing up, he slammed his head into the other kid's mouth, knocking out both of his front teeth. And this poor kid had just gotten his braces removed!

We rushed him to the bathroom and pushed his teeth back into his mouth, hoping they might reattach. And they actually did! It worked!

He did need to get braces again, though.

GERREN

My very first youth trip as a volunteer was at a conference hosted in a hotel. The pool at this hotel was amazing. It had two levels. The top level of the pool overflowed like a waterfall into the lower level of the pool, about three feet below.

I watched as one of our young adults jumped from the top level of the pool (which was six or seven feet deep) and flipped, landing gracefully in the lower level of the pool. I thought that looked pretty cool, so I decided to try a trick of my own.

I dove from the top level of the pool into the lower level. What I had failed to notice, though, was that the lower level of the pool was only three feet deep. I figured it out when I busted my face open on the bottom of the pool.

MARY JEAN

During our winter retreat, we were supposed to take our students bowling after our evening service. We piled all 50 kids onto the charter bus we had rented . . . but we couldn't find the bus driver.

My husband finally found the bus driver taking a nap in a nearby cabin and woke him up. The driver came running to the bus, looking very disheveled and sleepy, and started driving.

A few minutes later, the bus lurched, we all heard a huge crack, and the bus driver yelled, "OH, $#*&!"

He had missed his turn and attempted to turn around in what he thought was a large open parking lot. It wasn't a parking lot. It was a frozen retention pond.

Local firefighters had to carry our students out of the frozen pond on their backs, one by one. It was definitely an unforgettable youth ministry moment!

KEN

We took twenty-something teenagers on a mission trip to New York City for a week. The trip was great, but as we were trying to figure out how to navigate the subway system, I got a little tense. Figuring how and when to switch trains was a challenge.

At one point, I heard a commotion behind me and turned to see that one of my students had jumped down onto the rails! Yeah, the area with the highly electrified track and high-speed trains!

Fortunately, he was out just as quickly as he had jumped in. Apparently, teenagers will risk their actual lives to save their dropped phones.

I once took my youth group to a conference of around 5,000 students. We were staying in a dorm on the fifteenth floor. Throughout the conference, the line for the elevator was often incredibly long, so I would get pretty irritated when I saw kids using the elevator to get to the second or third floors instead of taking the stairs.

Toward the end of the conference, I hopped onto the elevator with a few of my students and a few strangers and saw that the button for Level 2 had been pressed. Pretty loudly, I said, "Floors four and under should really take the stairs."

From behind me, I heard someone say, "Yeah, we'd like to." It was an adult leader with a teenage girl in a wheelchair.

Longest one-floor elevator ride of my life.

MATTHEW

One week, our worship team was planning to perform the cheesy, super-sappy song "Christmas Shoes" as a joke. You know the one. It's about a little kid who wants to buy some shoes for his sick mom?

At the last minute, we realized a girl in the audience had just lost her mom to cancer. We pulled the plug on that one really quick.

So let's call this one an almost-fail.

Speaking of Christmas, I got in a lot of trouble once with a middle school mom. I was pretty new at being a middle school pastor and I was doing a series about faith. I thought I'd open the series with a funny story about the time I learned that Santa didn't exist.

That was the day I learned that some middle schoolers still believe in Santa.

MIKE

Our winter retreat was coming up when a parent contacted me. He owned a limousine company and wanted to donate a few limos to help our students get to camp so we could save money on buses. That sounded like a sweet deal to me, so I took him up on his offer.

When the vehicles arrived, I was told we would be receiving a few limos and one "party bus," whatever that meant. As students started piling in, I heard something I wasn't quite expecting to hear. One of my students poked his head out of the "party bus" and yelled, "Hey guys, look! This limo has a stripper pole!"

Needless to say, I got a call from my pastor on Monday morning.

We were wrapping up a series on sexual purity when we decided to split up the guys and girls for a couple of candid conversations about tough issues. I'm thinking the girls' conversation went a lot better than ours.

The guys' conversation was actually going really well. Until I said this . . .

"Pornography and masturbation are very real issues. Just know if this is something you struggle with, you don't have to walk alone. I'll come alongside you on your journey. Wait. That's not what I meant. I just mean I'm here to give you a hand. Nope. Don't mean that either. Uh. I think I might be fired."

BRYAN

My biggest fail in youth ministry was a mission trip to Haiti. Everything that could possibly have gone wrong went wrong.

It all started after our first flight. We had a layover in Miami, but flight delays caused us to miss it and forced us to spend the night in a hotel. By the time we got out of the airport, we only had three hours to sleep before needing to head back to the airport.

When we finally arrived in Haiti, there were bed bugs in every bed.

A few days into the trip, several girls weren't eating or drinking enough water, so they all got sick and weak. One of them passed out and hit her head. She'd had a concussion recently, so when she woke up she couldn't remember where she was or who we were.

Then, halfway through the trip, a riot broke out near our hotel, resulting in overturned vehicles, fires, and protests. On our way back to the hotel, we had to travel through the same area where those riots and protests were taking place.

When the week finally came to a close, we headed back to the airport. Our flights home were, of course, delayed. Then they were delayed some more. Finally, they were canceled completely.

We were able to catch a flight home with another airline, but unfortunately they were one seat short. I stayed an extra night in Haiti while the rest of my team flew home without me.

Oh boy. Craziest trip ever.

I grew up in the city, but my first youth ministry job was in a small farm town. I wasn't really sure what life in a small town was like exactly, but I wanted to do something that would connect with my students and maybe even draw some new ones.

My genius idea? Goat races.

We met at a school softball field. A local farmer showed up with his two goats. When we were ready to go, I told him to let them loose, expecting them to bolt, I guess?

They didn't. They just stood there. Then they ate some grass.

In an attempt to get them moving, one of my students tried chasing the goats. That certainly got them moving, but not in the way I was expecting. The male goat got a little, um, excited and mounted the female goat.

So much for that idea.

NATHAN

At some point, I decided it was time to delegate responsibility for our games to a volunteer. He had been with our ministry for a few years, so I trusted him.

One of the first games he put together was something called Veggie Pass. It was intended to be a race, where two competing teams passed a vegetable from one player to another using only their knees.

The vegetable he chose? A zucchini.

Yeah. Go ahead and picture that.

MATT

We once planned a Minute to Win It night for our middle schoolers, where we spent the whole night competing in up-front Minute-to-Win-It-style games. At the end of the night, I thought it would be fun to give our volunteers a chance to compete so students could cheer for their favorite leader.

The game selected for our leaders was called "Hanky Panky." As our leaders lined up to compete in the game, I introduced them one by one and asked our students who they thought was going to win.

One of our female leaders didn't get a ton of cheers, so to keep her spirits up, I said, "Come on, guys! Little do you know, she's a pro at Hanky Panky!"

It sounded better in my head.

DEDRA

A few years ago, I was assisting our youth minister with a weekend retreat. A few days before we were schedule to leave, he sent me a text asking if I was ready for the weekend.

In a hurry, I quickly texted him back: "Yes, I'm getting my thongs ready."

Things. I mean things.

AMANDA

This past summer, we took our students to Georgia for a mission trip. On the trip, we stopped for a quick Walmart run and told our students to be back out front in fifteen minutes.

At the end of fifteen minutes, we did a head count and jumped back into the vans.

Ten minutes later, we realized we had forgotten someone — our only student without a cell phone.

When we finally located him, he hadn't even realized we had left him behind. He was still shopping.

STEPHEN

It was 6:30am on my first high school guys' camping trip. Everyone was still a little groggy, which might be why we thought what happened next was a good idea.

A flock of birds was wading in the water nearby when someone had the brilliant idea to shoot at them with airsoft guns. Who knew an airsoft gun could knock a wing right off a bird?

Not my proudest moment.

TIFFANY

We were ready to head home at the end of a weekend rafting trip in a state park. I reached into my pocket to grab the van key and . . . it wasn't there.

We looked all over that state park for the key. At the lake. In the field. In the tents. In every piece of luggage. We looked *everywhere*.

When I finally made peace with the fact that the key was long gone, I called the church and someone met us 90 minutes away with an extra key.

Solution: I now carry a copy of the van key in my wallet at all times.

ROGER

Every year, we plan a week-long drama tour where we serve churches during the day and minister through drama during the evenings. One summer, I was approached by a Christian recording artist who had seen our team perform and wanted us to tour with them the following year. They set up some dates and locations with us and stayed in touch throughout the year.

The next summer, I confirmed and promoted the tour and we set out for our first gig.

Imagine my surprise when, after four hours of travel, the small ministry center we were visiting had no idea who we were or why we were there. Apparently, the recording artist we had been working with hadn't followed through on any of the bookings.

After some quick thinking and a few phone calls, I was able to salvage the trip and book a few last-minute ministry opportunities, but I learned a valuable lesson.

We played the game Bigger and Better at one of our events. You know, the one where every team starts with a paper clip and has to keep trading it for something bigger and better?

Well, I guess I should have stipulated that you couldn't bring back any living creatures because someone came back with a puppy.

His name is Cooper now. He lives with me.

HEATHER

One of my biggest fails in youth ministry was our summer trip. We were planning to take about 75 students to our denomination's bi-annual conference and then on a week-long missions experience.

As we were loading the buses, preparing to leave the conference and begin our mission experience, I was standing outside near the buses. When I looked up, I noticed our worship pastor's daughter had her face pressed against the window and was making faces at me. I thought it would be funny to give her a little scare, so I jumped up and smacked her window with my hand.

Apparently I hit that window a little too hard though, because the force broke the girl's front tooth in half. Whoops!

Back when I was joining my church staff as the junior high pastor, our high school pastor had a great idea to serve the community. He asked the local township how we could help them and they asked us to collect everyone's extra or unused paint cans, since they needed to be disposed of in a special facility.

We mobilized the whole church to distribute flyers to the community. The following week, we rolled out in trucks and collected over 2,000 paint cans. It was awesome. We were all super pumped about serving the community in a tangible way.

That is . . . until we found out it would cost $5.00 per paint can to dispose of everything. That's a fact the township conveniently forgot to share with us.

For six months, our youth room was filled with paint cans.

BRIAN

Since we share a campus with a local Christian school, we have access to their great cafe and professional food service equipment, including a warming oven that we use for pizza.

We used that warming oven for years without incident. But as our event attendance grew, we had to start ordering more and more pizzas. Last year, I guess we added one too many pizzas to the warming oven. One of the cardboard boxes made contact with the heating element in the warmer and started on fire.

As parents were dropping off their students, the building started filling with smoke. We had to clear 300 students and 50 volunteers from the building and wait for the fire department to give us the all-clear before going back inside.

And the worst part? We had to replace all the pizza.

LAURA BETH

My husband and I were chaperoning a weekend Bible study retreat with fifteen of our students alongside nine other youth groups. It was a great weekend!

On our last night, all ten of our groups took a dinner cruise together to celebrate. Unbeknownst to us, two of our guys set their sights on a cute girl from another group and made a "slap bet" to see who could get her number first. The winner would get to slap the loser as hard as he could.

One of the boys successfully got the girl's number, but when the winning boy tried to claim his winnings, the other boy told my husband and me about the bet and pleaded with us to protect him.

We didn't. We let the slap happen. It was a pretty good slap, too.

CALLIE

One night, I was driving a few high schoolers to an event when I saw a flock of geese up ahead, running toward the road. I thought about it for a second and concluded, "If I were a goose, I would stop and look both ways before I walked into the middle of a busy road."

I was wrong.

The kids in my car claim I mercilessly crushed the life out of those geese as feathers and carnage flew everywhere. I like to say the geese hit *me*. Not my fault.

COURTNEY

At our summer high school camp, I took a group of girls to a natural hot spring for one of our cabin discussions.

One of the girls said, "I'm so hot, I feel like my legs are melting."

I intended to make a cool movie reference and say, "Do you feel like a Nazi, like in *Indiana Jones*, when their faces melt off?"

Unfortunately, the girls cut me off after the word "Nazi" and harassed me about my supposed insensitivity.

As it turns out, sentence structure can be pretty important.

TRACY

My biggest fail happened during an all-nighter. We had gone to a bowling alley, bowled for a couple of hours, then returned to the church so we could give away some prizes to our bowling champions. It was about 2:30am.

While I was on stage, my phone rang. I didn't recognize the number. Trying to be funny, I answered the phone, put it on speaker, and held it up to the microphone.

It was the mom of one of our students. She was calling to say we had left her son at the bowling alley.

I felt horrible. But, in my defense, his own brother didn't notice he was missing either.

STEPHEN

I live in a small town. The parsonage, where I live, is right across the street from the high school. One year, on graduation night, I had a great idea.

It's pretty common for church people to park in our front lawn for school events, and there were plenty of cars there that night. I thought it would be fun to climb into the back of one of my students' cars, then jump out and scare them to death when the time was right. I found my victim's vehicles, climbed into her SUV, turned everything on (the radio at full volume, the windshield wipers, the heat — everything) and hunkered down in the far back row, ready to jump out and scare her when the time was right . . . except the three people who climbed into the car were complete strangers. And they were all pretty elderly.

I watched in horror from the backseat as the elderly man climbed into the driver's seat and started the car. It was just as chaotic as I'd planned, but instead of jumping out and scaring them, I cowered in the back, thinking, "I'm going to kill these people. I am going to give them all heart attacks and they are going to die. I'm a murderer."

Once the driver got the windshield wipers, radio, and head under control, I sat up very slowly. With the most soothing voice I could muster, I said, "Hello there. I'm Pastor Stephen. I live here."

Needless to say, they were pretty surprised.

That's when I realized I couldn't get out of the car from the inside. I had to wait for my wife to come outside and let me out through the back window.

IYA

We were on a youth retreat in the Outer Banks. It was a hot day and I was responsible for organizing the games for our middle schoolers. The game I had chosen for that day was Egg Roulette, a game where you smash eggs over your own head — most are hard-boiled, but some are raw.

We had six large cartons of eggs for the retreat, but in preparation for the game, we hard boiled two-thirds of one of the cartons. When it was time to play, I grabbed the partially cooked carton . . . or so I thought.

As it turns out, I grabbed a carton of entirely raw eggs. As soon as the students realized what had happened, it turned into an all-out egg war.

There was a hose nearby, but do you have any idea what egg-soaked teenagers smell like after a day of playing in the hot sun?

Let me tell you about the day I thought I was going to be fired.

When I was brand new to youth ministry, I wanted to use secular music as a tool to break down barriers with new students. I planned an outreach night that was going to open with our band covering a few secular songs.

I was leading the first song: "Boulevard of Broken Dreams," by Green Day. As we began to play, I suddenly realized a few things.

First, this song had an f-bomb in it. Second, our tech volunteer was putting the lyrics on the screen. And third, I had not read over those slides.

I learned a lot that day. I didn't get fired, but I don't use Green Day songs in my youth services more either.

JEFFREY

We were in the airport headed out of the country for a mission trip when a student told me he didn't have his passport with him. I assumed he meant it was in his luggage, so I assured him it would be fine — I figured he could board with just his license and we could deal with customs after we landed and retrieved his passport from his luggage.

Ten days later, we were headed back into the US, just a few feet from the border, when the same student reminded me he didn't have his passport. That's when I realized, *Oh! He didn't have his passport at all.* He didn't even bring it!

We prayed and sweat for twenty minutes until we finally reached the border. Thankfully, in this one instance, the border security agents let us slide through. I've never been so relieved.

JASMINE

We recently started planning our own youth camps. One of the things we love doing at camp is to put our students in teams. We give them team names and then let them create their own team flags.

We thought we had come up with some pretty cool team names, including one team called The Knock-Out Kings.

When our teams started working on their team flags, however, we found The Knock-Out Kings cracking up in the corner. Turns out, they were laughing about the nickname they had given themselves: The KOK's, which, when said phonetically . . . you get the picture.

We retired that team name after that.

RYAN

Our students nagged and nagged me to plan a lock-in for them. Finally, I gave in.

Thirty-five students showed up, which was great! My intern and I were hanging out upstairs watching a movie with some of our high schoolers when, suddenly, I woke up.

I don't know how long I'd been asleep but when I opened my eyes, my intern was also asleep and the high schoolers had disappeared. In fact, several of them had walked to a gas station to buy Red Bulls while we slept.

Fortunately, nothing was broken and the high schoolers came right back, but still. I'm never doing a lock-in again.

JASON

My students and I were packed into a fifteen passenger van, riding high on the way home from an amazing weekend retreat. After an incredible weekend and some silly games in the van, my students were feeling pretty enthusiastic. A few high schoolers quickly made a sign that said, "Honk if you love Jesus!" They held the sign up to the window and made it their mission to get at least twenty honks before we made it home.

When we got to ten honks, another vehicle pulled up alongside us. They had made a sign of their own and were trying to get us to read it. I assumed the sign said something similar to ours, so I started honking the horn wildly, excited to have found some fellow believers on the road. Over and over again, I honked and honked and honked.

That's when I realized everyone in my van, as well as the car beside us, were laughing hysterically. The sign the other car was holding said, "Honk if you love weed."

SEAN

We were playing a game called Anatomy Clump, where you call out a number and a body part (like "three elbows" or "twenty-five toes") and your students have to clump together accordingly.

For some reason, I thought it was a good idea to call out, "four booties." Everyone scrambled around the room, trying to clump into groups of four, when I noticed one girl was still running around, trying to find a group.

That's when I yelled into the microphone, "Oooh, Carlee's looking for some booty!"

She froze.
I froze.
Everyone froze.

And then everyone erupted in laughter.

CALEB

After a great day of swimming with my students, everyone was hungry (big surprise). We couldn't decide where to eat, so we split up into two groups. I took a few students one way while one of my leaders took the rest of the students another way.

When we were done eating, I called my leader to find out where they had gone.

Turns out he had gone to Hooters. With our students. In the church van.

ROBBY

One year, we hosted a Super Bowl party. There were lots of snacks, of course, including a huge bowl of pretzels. When the pretzels were gone, there was a huge handful of salt at the bottom of the bowl. I called out, "Hey! Who's going to finish this salt?"

A student volunteered and we cheered him on as he downed every bit of salt in that bowl.

Fifteen minutes later, I couldn't find him. Turns out he had been in the bathroom throwing up. I guess you're not supposed to eat that much salt at one time.

GARRETT

In my first year of ministry, the middle schoolers and I were playing with Nerf guns outside. I even hopped into my Jeep and drove it slowly around the parking lot like a dart-slinging tank! It was awesome . . . until we were stopped by a cop.

It gets worse.

While the officer stood with me in the parking lot, telling me how irresponsible my actions were, an eighth grader jumped into my Jeep, put it into reverse, and nearly ran over the officer and me.

DANIEL

We tried a game once involving pantyhose that didn't go very well. Here's the idea: you take a set of pantyhose, cut it in half so you have two separate legs, put some type of ball in the foot of each leg, and then put them over two students' heads, kind of like an elephant trunk. The goal of the game is to wrap your "trunk" around your opponents' "trunk" and rip the pantyhose off their head.

Apparently, it matters what type of ball you put in the end of the pantyhose and the ball I chose may have been a little too heavy.

Within thirty seconds of the start of the game, one of my tenth grade guys got hit in the face. His nose bled everywhere. And then he started crying.

STEPHEN

We also played a pantyhose game, with more unfortunate results. In this game, students put pantyhose over their faces while standing back to back with their opponents. Then we tied the feet of their pantyhose together. At the count of three, they were supposed to run in opposite directions as they tried to yank off their opponents' pantyhose.

Well, the pantyhose we purchased must have had extra small waistbands because those things were really difficult to yank off once they were over someone's head.

Our first round resulted in a student being dragged a few feet across the carpet by his neck. As he fell, he managed to stick his hand between his neck and the waistband of the stocking, but he ended up with a sprained wrist and carpet burn covering his entire forearm.

One night during youth group, I tossed a pizza (still in its cardboard box) into the oven to keep it warm. The oven must have been a little bit too hot though, because a few minutes later, every fire alarm in the church was blaring.

Our fire alarm system automatically notifies the local fire department of an emergency, so I quickly got on the phone to let them know we were fine and not to bother sending a truck. They said they were having a slow night, so they were going to head over anyway.

Long after the beeping had stopped and the pizza box had been removed from the oven, five fire trucks pulled in, fire fighters poured into the building like ants at a picnic, oxygen tanks and axes at the ready.

While they cleared the building and checked every fire extinguisher, my students and I had to wait outside. In the rain. For twenty minutes.

JANETH

About three years into our ministry, my husband and I planned a beach trip. As usual, we had some difficulty finding enough people to help us drive, so we borrowed a small RV from someone in our church.

We had a great day, but on the way back to the church I noticed the RV was beginning to slow down. The next thing I knew, there were flames bursting out from the radio. We quickly pulled to the side of the freeway and evacuated the RV. Within minutes, the entire thing was engulfed in flames!

The fire department arrived, traffic backed up, and other drivers jumped out of their cars to check on us and bring our students water bottles. Thank God no one was hurt!

JENNA

It was my first day doing announcements as a youth ministry intern. My job that day was supposed to be pretty simple. All I needed to do was invite our students to participate in a Christmas giving project called Angel Tree.

Unfortunately, I pronounced it "Anal Tree."

CARLA

We once played a game that involved covering our small group leaders' faces in maple syrup and letting their students throw Cheerios at them to see how many they could get to stick.

The students loved it. The leaders? Not so much. Half of them spent the next thirty minutes in the bathroom trying to get their eyelids unstuck.

ANDREW

We recently did a series about sex with our middle schoolers, but I didn't exactly do a great job preparing my small group leaders for the series. Unfortunately, this led to our fifth and sixth graders asking some pretty difficult questions about sex . . . and a few of my college-aged leaders sharing a little too much information about their, um, *experience* with the topic.

Let's just say I had a lot of phone calls from parents to return that week.

In my first year pastoring my middle schoolers, we were talking about Jesus' birth. I had a few pretty skeptical eighth grade girls in my group who wanted to debate whether or not the virgin birth really happened. After all, she said, there are other ways to get pregnant besides sex, like in vitro fertilization. At this point, I wanted to get our conversation back on track, so I reminded her that IVF is a very modern procedure and I was pretty sure "no turkey basters" were involved with Jesus' birth.

That's when I noticed the bewildered look on the face of one of my sheltered little homeschooled girls.

Note to self: maybe don't get into group debates about Jesus' conception until all of your students have had the sex talk.

ELLE

For a few years, I volunteered in our middle school and high school ministries at the same time. Since our programs were on different days, there usually wasn't a conflict. One week, though, I spent an entire sleepless weekend on a retreat with my high schoolers, then woke up early on Sunday morning to help with the middle school service.

When I got there, I was asked to help with a game. We were doing human bowling, where we put students on scooters, launched them at cardboard targets, and then intercepted them before they slammed face-first into a wall. My job was to intercept them.

Unfortunately, I was very tired. I walked to my post and, as I waited for the game to begin, thought about the incredible nap I was going to take that afternoon. Then I heard two things: a loud *BOOM!* and the entire room say, "Ooohhhh." The game had started. A sixth grader had just shot past me on a scooter and slammed straight into the wall.

DANIEL

On every mission trip, I try to do one fun thing during our trip. On one of our trips, I decided to take our students kayaking. The activity was going great . . . until we hit a bend in the river. The current was going so fast that my kayak slammed me into the river wall so hard that my kayak flipped and my prescription glasses fell into the water, never to be found again.

Unfortunately, I was the only person old enough to drive our rented van and we still had a four hour drive ahead of us. Without my glasses, I had to have a student sit in the front seat and tell me when I was getting too close to the other cars on the road.

When we got back to the site where we were staying, a volunteer had an extra pair of prescription glasses. Unfortunately, they were rose-tinted sunglasses. I had to wear those things every minute for the rest of the trip.

SETH

When I first got married, there was a girl in my youth group who looked a lot like my wife. Like, a *lot*. One night on our mission trip, I was sitting next to my wife with my arm around the back of her chair. I momentarily leaned away from my wife to talk to a student. When I turned back toward her, I leaned in for a kiss when I realized . . . that wasn't my wife. In the brief moment I had turned away, she had gotten up and my look-alike student had sat down. Fortunately, I realized my mistake before anything really creepy happened.

Flustered, I wanted to make a joke about how much this student dressed like my wife. Unfortunately, I phrased it like this: "She totally wants to be my wife."

As my students later informed me, that made me sound like both a pervert and a polygamist.

HILARY

I'm small. Like, really small. Some of my middle schoolers are even taller than me. I have one middle schooler who is significantly taller than me and likes to pick me up or push me around when she's really excited and wants my attention. It's pretty irritating and she knows it.

One week, I'd had it. She repeatedly pushed me toward a couch during small group time and I snapped. I reprimanded her, in front of her entire small group, with more gusto than I had ever used toward a student before.

That's when I realized the entire small group was staring at me. This girl had been directing me to the couch so she and her small group could give me a special gift as a way to say thank you for investing in them that year. They had been planning it for weeks.

ROB

One week, we gave our students a challenge. Whoever could drink a glass of kale juice the fastest would be the winner. Sure, it's kind of gross, but kale is good for you, right?

Well, the night ended with a number of my girls experiencing significant stomach pain. One even puked on the youth room floor.

TREVOR

I once used cow liver for a gross game. The game was great but after the service I realized I needed to figure out how to get rid of it.

I could have thrown it away, but then I'd have to take out the trash, which seemed like a hassle. Then I realized I might be able to flush it down the toilet. I was smart enough to realize the entire liver wouldn't fit down the toilet, so I started ripping it apart with my fingers. Unfortunately, I dropped it directly into the toilet. It seemed to slide down the pipes pretty easily though, so I thought I was in the clear. I flushed . . . and immediately realized I had clogged the toilet.

I tried a plunger. It didn't work. I tried a coat hanger. Nope. I even got a plumber's snake. That didn't work either. Eventually, I found myself at Walmart at midnight telling an employee I needed new parts for my toilet because I had clogged it trying to flush a liver. He was a little suspicious, but he helped me out anyway.

When I was a nineteen-year-old intern, I was working late one night and walked into the parking lot to grab something from my car. While I was out there, a woman in a minivan pulled up to ask me for directions to the church's main office.

I gave her directions, but no matter how I described how to get there, this woman did not seem to understand what I was saying. I was really frustrated, but I tried to keep it cool.

When I got back to the office, I told two of my co-workers about what had happened. I went on and on about how annoying it was that this woman could not understand me. I thought it was a little weird that my co-workers were just staring at me in silence, but I kept going anyway.

Then I turned around. The woman from the parking lot had been standing behind me the entire time.

MARK

We let our students help choose the theme for some of our events by writing their ideas down on scraps of paper. One year, we got a suggestion for a theme that had to do with pants. I'll spare you the exact wording, but the paper said, "_____ Pants Nights." The word I have kindly edited out for you was a word none of our adults had never heard before. We tried for weeks to figure out what it meant, but we couldn't find the word or phrase anywhere. We ultimately decided it was a nickname for Spongebob Square Pants and so it was safe to use as an event theme. Bad choice.

We planned our entire event around the theme of pants. We planned pants-related games, created pants-themed graphics, and prepared a message about being clothed in righteousness. We even wrote "_____ Pants Night" on all of our flyers.

A few days before the event, we finally figured out what that phrase meant: premature ejaculation.

MEGAN

One night, we played a game involving uncooked spaghetti noodles. After the game, some of the students kept a noodle or two to chew on or use to stab each other.

As we transitioned into worship, I grabbed the microphone and exclaimed, "Okay everyone, come on up for worship. Leave everything in your chairs. I don't need you guys playing with your noodles while we worship."

In a room full of teenage boys, that didn't go over very well.

One week into my role at a new church, I had the great idea to film a video outside at night. I gave our students washable spray paint and let them graffiti my car while I filmed it. Then we headed inside.

A few minutes later, the cops showed up. Apparently someone had reported a man and some teenagers tagging cars in the church parking lot.

CRAIG

One snowy November night, I had to intervene in an argument between a high school couple that had just broken up. The guy was pretty upset, so I told him to go outside and cool down. He stormed toward the door, cursing, so I called after him, "Change your attitude or walk home!"

Well . . . he walked. In the snow. For five miles. Without a jacket.

Reminder: if you don't mean it, don't say it.

TRACY

My husband and I once took our students on a mission trip out of state. We wanted to be extremely prepared, so we packed a backpack with every medical form and all of our students' medications, plus we brought two sets of keys to the van.

When we stopped for dinner, we accidentally locked the backpack and both sets of keys inside the van. So much for preparation.

It was already 9:00pm, but it was hours before the fire department arrived (with a ladder truck, lights on) along with AAA and let us back into the van.

LISA

We do an annual event called Sleep Out for the Homeless, where our students stand along the street outside our church and use milk jugs to collect money from passing cars. It's a great event that helps raise both funds and awareness for local agencies that help those struggling with homelessness.

One year, I was asked to tell the children in our church about the event. I'm more comfortable talking with teenagers, so it was a little bit of a struggle to figure out how to talk on the level of little kids.

My "kid-friendly" explanation of this event ended up sounding something like this: "We stand on the street corner and shake our jugs for money."

A youth pastor friend of mine really hates lock-ins. For a long time, he refused to do them at his church, until his students started really begging him to make one happen.

Finally, he relented and told his college interns they could do one but that he wouldn't be there. Since the target group of students was relatively small, he let the interns use the youth ministry office building for the event, since there were couches and futons available. All seemed to be according to plan, so the students and interns went to sleep.

When they woke up, they weren't alone.

During the night, a homeless man had wandered in and fallen asleep on a futon — right next to a middle school boy.

Apparently, the interns had forgotten to lock the doors.

JILEEN

We all know it's hard to keep up with some of the latest phrases and terminology, but my friend Josh had a pretty awkward slip-up recently.

After a snowy weekend, Josh opened the service like this: "Hey guys, how was your weekend? Pretty low-key? What'd you guys do? Netflix and chill?"

Blank stares.
Silence.
Awkward laughter.

That was the day we taught Josh about Urban Dictionary.

Okay, this was my absolute worst moment in youth ministry. I had a student in my ministry who loved letting his boxers hang out of his pants. It was pretty excessive. He was constantly showing them off.

One day, in front of his mom, I told him that if he kept letting his boxers hang out, I might have to pants him one of these days.

Well, that day came. While we were hanging out in our youth room, I grabbed his pants and pulled. Unfortunately, I had also grabbed his boxers. The entire room saw his butt.

Please, never pants a student. Ever. Please.

MELISSA

When I was three months into my current job, I planned a tacky Christmas party for our students. After some image searching, I found a picture of a tacky Christmas sweater with a snowman on it, turned it into a flyer, and sent the flyers home with our students two or three weeks before the party.

The day of the party, I got a call from my senior pastor. He told me a concerned parent had called about the party. I panicked. "Have a look at your flyer," he said, "and call me back."

How do I put this? The snowman on my flyer had been decorated with two carrots. And one of those carrots was not on its face.

Back when Halo was still really new and popular, I hosted a lock-in for about thirty guys to play Halo all night long. My assistant and I were the only adults.

At around 2:00am, I went into my office . . . and went to sleep. I have no idea what happened that night.

At least it wasn't a co-ed lock-in?

CARLA

My brother Shawn is a volunteer in our ministry. Over the span of three short months, Shawn dislocated his shoulder, broke his toe, and got a concussion — all from games we played in our youth group. After the concussion, he had to take three weeks off from work and four months to heal completely.

Our students eventually created a board in the youth room where they kept track of how many weeks we could go without injuring Shawn. He got through an entire semester uninjured . . . but an incident at our kick-off bash sent him back to zero.

Earlier in my career, I got it into my head that every cool youth pastor should be able to play guitar, so I tried teaching myself how to play.

Once I had a few songs under my belt, I decided to finally start a time of weekly worship with my students, which I'd been wanting to do for quite a while.

It wasn't until I started to play and sing that I realized I wasn't actually good at either playing or singing. My rhythm was off and I was totally terrible. My leaders tried to sing extra loud to drown me out.

I didn't try that again.

KATE

This was a year of firsts for me!

It was my first year as a full-time youth pastor.

This summer was my first time driving a group of students to summer camp.

It was also my first time getting a speeding ticket . . . while driving said students to summer camp.

CATHY

Our annual girls' summer lock-in is a great time for girls to laugh, be themselves, and get to know each other. Sometimes I think the atmosphere leaves me acting a little bit more like a teenager than I usually would.

One year, it rained like crazy, to the point where our rickety old building started to leak. The entire kitchen floor was covered in rain water. When we discovered it, I decided it would be fun to run and slide across the water with my bare feet.

I managed it just fine, but a teenage girl decided to give it a try too. When she did, her feet flew out from under her and she slammed her head on the tile floor. Hard.

Not only was she concussed, but she hit her head so hard the impact burst her eardrum. I still see that moment in my nightmares.

In my early days of youth ministry, I never considered the perspective of my students' parents. This was never so obvious as the Wednesday night I decided to take all of my students cliff jumping.

Our weekly turnout was lower than usual that day, so instead of doing youth group, I figured swimming and jumping off a few rocks would be more fun. I piled all of my students into my van and took off for the cliffs.

Fortunately, nothing terrible happened, but I never told my students' parents where we were going or asked for their permission.

On one of my first youth trips at my previous church, our van broke down. I called my pastor to let him know and he told me to call AAA. So I did!

Except I dialed incorrectly and ended up calling an "adult" line.

MATT

For my first ever lock-in, I was running an all-night 30 Hour Famine event, where students fast for thirty hours to raise money and awareness for people in need.

I planned a ton of events to keep our students occupied throughout the night . . . but, on the night of the event, none of my volunteers showed up. Every single adult canceled on me. Plus, the events I planned took way less time than I anticipated, so we were done with all of our programming by 11:00pm.

The result? I was locked in a building all night with group of hungry, bored teenagers. Alone.

JERRY

Our church is located in an area of our city that was once referred to as "The War Zone." It's known for its high rates of poverty, homelessness, human trafficking, and crime. When I joined the team as the youth pastor, I tried to be very intentional about loving and respecting everyone who walked through our doors.

One of my first weeks on the job, a few interesting-looking girls walked into our youth service. They looked a little too old to be there, but I wasn't sure and didn't want to presume. When my security guards arrived, they laughed at me. Those girls were not girls. They were adults. And they were males. Apparently, these folks were well known in the community as cross-dressers and they were most definitely not in high school. When they tried volunteering for a game, I had to let them know this was a teenagers-only service.

ERIK

We once planned an outreach event where we offered a $50 gift card for the student who brought the most friends. Well, that incentive worked a little too well. We had planned for 125 students, but ended up with more than 300. This was amazing, of course, but a logistical nightmare.

We didn't have enough seats on the bus we had rented, so we crammed every single student we could onto that bus . . . with only one adult. After being pushed, screamed at, and having things thrown at her, that poor woman came to me crying as soon as they arrived at our destination: a farm for hayrides.

Since we had planned for 125 students, we had rented three trucks and filled them with hay bales. Each truck was designed to hold 50 students. Instead, we crammed nearly 100 students onto each truck.

We did what we could to make it work and, as it turned out, we had 23 students make first-time decisions for Jesus, so that was a huge win! Unfortunately, when I got back to the office on Monday, I (rightfully) had a mountain of complaints to sift through, including a five -page handwritten letter about how incompetent I was.

That was twenty years ago and it still stings a little, but I learned some really valuable lessons from that event.

Once a year, our denomination's regional university would rent out Six Flag and sell tickets just for our special event. For a whole night, we got the park completely to ourselves. It was awesome. Plus, every ticket to this event came with an additional free ticket that could be redeemed at a future date.

A youth pastor friend of mine told me that, the year before, he had sold their extra free tickets the next morning as a fund raiser for his youth group. I thought that was a pretty good idea, so I tried it. The morning after the event, I drove to Six Flags with my extra tickets in hand and sold a few of them right away. I turned toward a woman who I thought was next in line to buy my tickets. She wasn't.

She was park security. She took me into park custody, took my mug shot, gave me a citation for scalping tickets, and banned me from the park for a year. The charges were eventually dropped, but still. Don't try to scalp Six Flags tickets, people.

When our newest batch of middle schoolers moved up into our ministry, we played the game Two Truths and a Lie to get to know each other. As I was explaining the game, I said, "Be sure to make your lies believable. Don't write something stupid like, 'I only have four toes.' No one will believe that."

When we collected the cards and read them out loud, I got to one card that said, "I only have nine fingers."

"Guys," I said, "Who wrote this? I told you not to write stupid things that aren't believable."

A new middle school girl raised her hand and said, "That was me. And it's true. I lost one of my fingers to cancer."

I wanted to curl up in a ball and die.

STEPHEN

Once, I was helping a fellow youth pastor with a guys' retreat. We went rafting down a river one afternoon with students and leaders in three different rafts. Suddenly, a high school student fell out of his raft and didn't surface. After a few seconds, we realized he couldn't swim and he wasn't wearing a life jacket.

I quickly jumped in and held him above water until someone got him a life jacket. He was fine and was even joking about it.

Later, I was messing around with a younger middle school guy and pushed him off the raft. As he was falling into the water, I realized my mistake. He was the younger brother of the first guy who had fallen into the water. And he couldn't swim either.

MATT

When I was studying youth ministry in college, my school hosted a conference for high schoolers that we got to run.

During one of the late night sessions, my friend and I hosted a variety show for all 3,000 students. A group of freshman girls had just performed a crazy tumbling routine, when my co-host said, "I bet you can't do a flip like those girls did, Matt."

Of course, my ego kicked in, so I walked to the edge of the stage and attempted to do a back flip onto the floor. It didn't exactly go as planned. In reality, I did more of an awkward slow-motion whale-flop and landed flat on my face.

No one even laughed. It was that embarrassing.

CHAD

Our annual middle school fall retreat had just begun and it was, of course, chaos. When we got into our bunks, our leaders were supposed to meet with their rooms to talk about rules and expectations for the weekend . . . but one of our rookie leaders missed the memo. While he was who-knows-where, his boys were trying to decide how to prank him. You know what they came up with? A student walked into the leader's closet. And then he peed on the floor.

It wasn't just word of the prank that spread. It was the smell too.

Once we found the culprit, I made him clean it up. Unfortunately, we didn't really have any cleaning supplies handy, so we used hand soap and paper towels. After a few minutes of scrubbing, the combination of suds and pee somehow made the smell even worse.

It was pretty gross.

To promote our annual leader's meeting, I once dressed up like Adele and recreated her latest album cover. The cover of the invitation had that picture of me, along with the words, "Hello, it's me. I'm wondering if after all this time you'd like to meet to go over everything."

Unfortunately, almost no one understood the reference. They all just thought it was a weird sepia-toned picture of their youth pastor wearing a fur coat and staring off into the distance.

One of my small group leaders and I once took a group of twenty kids to a concert about an hour and a half away from home. I drove a 15-passenger van and my leader drove his own van with the rest of the students. The plan was to eat dinner at whatever concession stands were available at the concert but, when we arrived, we discovered a recent wrestling tournament had completely obliterated the school's food stash. The only things they had available were candy and Diet Sprite.

We were too late to come up with another plan, so we endured the concert on empty stomachs. Around midnight, we were back in our vans finally searching for something to eat. We were starving.

We found a Wendy's, but since it was midnight, only the drive-thru window was operating. As we pulled up to the speaker, I apologized in advance for what I knew was about to be a nightmare of an order. Imagine a van full of fifteen starving middle schoolers simultaneously screaming their orders at you through the partially-opened windows of a 15-passenger van. Understandably, the drive-thru operator immediately became confused. After several painful minutes, I made everyone get out of the van and line up. I asked the woman to please erase everything we had already accomplished and start again.

One at a time, I made the students walk up to the menu, squat down near the speaker, place their orders, and then get back into the van in an orderly fashion.

In what I can only describe as a miracle, when we finally got our food, every order was perfect. It was a very happy conclusion to a former fail of a day.

TIM

On one of my first trips with my current youth group, we were heading to a fall retreat in a caravan of vehicles — including a few that didn't run very well. About an hour into the trip, our old blue church van caught fire. The driver immediately pulled over to the first safe location he could find.

Unfortunately, that location was the parking lot of an adult book store. That's where we hung out, with all sixty teenagers, until we figured out a new plan for transportation.

When I was new to the Detroit area, I was planning to take a student to a hockey game for his birthday but, unfortunately, I missed a pretty important turn. Suddenly, I realized we were no longer in Michigan. We were on the bridge to Canada with no passports and no place to turn around. I panicked, imagining how this student's mom was going to react.

Luckily, after a lot of conversations and some paperwork, we were kindly escorted back in the good ol' United States.

I once turned on a movie for our preteens at an overnight event. I had seen the movie before and thought it was appropriate — after all, it was rated PG. Then I left the room for a few minutes. When I came back, our little preteens were staring open-mouthed at a scene involving a very drunken bar fight.

I guess I forgot about that part.

For my first summer as a middle school pastor, I wanted to do something big and fun. One Wednesday, I told everyone to wear clothes they wouldn't mind ruining. Then I went to Walmart and bought everything gross I could think of: chocolate syrup, pigs feet, anchovies, ketchup, mustard, peanut butter, and two kiddie pools filled with green slime.

I did have a structured program in mind but, once the students arrived, it quickly turned into complete chaos. I finally regained some control when I pulled out the slime pools. I had hidden some small objects in the pools and the game was to dive in and retrieve them, using only their mouths. And they did. Pretty enthusiastically.

Here's where the fail comes in. As students pulled their heads out of the green slime pools, I had a sickening realization: the green food coloring I had used was staining everyone's hair and skin green.

One year during our summer mission trip, we closed each night by writing funny memories and stories from the day on a bed sheet with permanent markers. It was a fun tradition that my students loved.

A few weeks after the mission trip, I had the opportunity to share some highlights from our trip with the whole congregation. I intended to say, "Every night, we would all sit together on a sheet and reflect on the day."

Instead, from the pulpit, I said, "Every night, we would all $#*! together on a seat."

MELISSA

I once took thirty-eight students to New York City on a mission trip. My assistant at the time booked train tickets for the entire group that would take us from Ohio to New York City and back.

After nine days in New York, we got ready to board our train home. My assistant went inside to get the tickets . . . but never came out. After a very long time, I went inside to find her. We found her curled in a ball on the floor of the train station. Our tickets, we learned, had been for the day before. They were non-refundable, we had no money left in our budget, and the next train was two days from then.

It was completely my fault for not double-checking the tickets but my assistant was mortified. She quit on the spot and I never saw her again. Seriously. How did we get home? I called in a favor from a friend who worked at a travel company and managed to find us all bus tickets. For $5,000.

DANIELLE

We once invited a guest band to lead our students in worship. The lead singer was an old college friend of mine. During worship, he was in the middle of an exhortation when he looked at me and asked if he was allowed to use "bad words" during church.

I assumed he wanted to know if he could say "crap" or "sucks," which would have been fine with me, so I just chuckled and told him to go for it.

Then he swore. Like, really swore. Repeatedly. He called it "real talk."

I was mortified and had to send a mass apology email the following day.

RICH

Please, don't ever, ever open a bathroom door without knocking. I once approached a single-stall bathroom in our church that I was positive was vacant. I put my ear to the door to listen for activity, but I didn't knock. When I opened it, lo and behold, there were three middle school girls inside, silently doing their hair and makeup. I thanked God repeatedly that's all I walked in on.

JESSE

In my first year of ministry, I had just taken over a junior high group and had planned a trip to a huge youth conference. Before we left, I decided to take all our guys shopping for new baseball hats, thinking it would be easier to keep track of them if they were all wearing matching hats. We purchased twelve hats — blue with gray bills.

Once we made it to the conference, I took the same group of guys on a train ride to get some lunch. We found a McDonalds in a nearby city, ate, and rode back to the hotel.

When we got back, my pastor asked where we had gone. When I told him, he pulled me aside to let me know I had just taken a group of junior highers into one of the most dangerous parts of the entire city . . . and I had dressed them all in the colors of a notorious local gang.

SHAWN

My very first time preaching, I was asked to teach at my former youth group about David and Bathsheba. (Looking back, I now wonder if that was just my old youth pastor messing with me.)

In my talk, I wanted to discuss the battle we face between our flesh and the Spirit within us. Just then, I got a little tongue-tied and stumbled over my words. What I ultimately said was this: "When David saw Bathsheba in that bath tub, something started to rise up."

Uhhhh.

The youth pastor and the adult leaders were laughing so hard they had to leave the room.

I once took a group of students on a mission trip to help a brand new church plant with its launch. After a long week of hard work, we decided to take the afternoon off, so I packed up our students, did a little research, and found what sounded like a really nice secluded beach.

When we got there, we realized why it was so secluded. I had just taken all of my students to a nude beach.

DANIEL

I once had a brilliant idea while planning a spring lock-in. Instead of playing boring old dodgeball, I thought we could play . . . *strobe light dodgeball*. I was picturing the most epic game of stop-motion dodgeball ever played. Pretty good idea, right? I picked up five industrial strobe lights, set them up in our gym, and tested them out the day of the event. I was positive this game was going to be amazing. Spoiler alert: it wasn't.

Once the sun had gone down and all the lights were turned off, it was dark — like, pitch dark. In comparison, the brightness of the strobe lights was completely blinding. And to make matters worse, once the strobe lights were plugged in there was no way to sync up the timing of all five lights.

The result was complete chaos. There were head-on collisions. Everyone (even people who weren't playing) got hit in the face with stray balls. Students got vertigo and had to lie down so they didn't puke. *Never again.*

JOSH

We were on our way home from our first trip to summer camp when my biggest fail happened. In the middle of our 4-hour drive home, we pulled into a gas station to hit the bathrooms. Even though there were only two stalls, my students were out in record time, so I rewarded them with a trip into the gas station to grab snacks.

30 minutes later, one of my boys said he had to go to the bathroom *again*. I told him no way. He had just gone to and now there was nowhere to stop, so he would have to hold it. A few minutes later, it was clear he wasn't going to make it. Quickly, we pulled over to the side of the road. He jumped out, ran to the edge of the woods at the edge of the highway, and started peeing into the trees. This apparently served as a trigger for every other boy on the bus because, suddenly, all ten of my middle school boys were lined up on the side of the road, late at night, peeing on trees together while the girls stayed on the bus and screamed.

RANDY

One winter I decided to do something a little different with my students: a winter picnic! The weather seemed fine enough, but this native Texan was, I guess, not totally accustomed to the winters of Nebraska, where I was serving at the time.

On the day of the picnic, the weather turned icy, the wind turned blustery, and the high was around five degrees Fahrenheit. This is a fail story, so of course I didn't cancel it. Five kids showed up, three stayed in the car the entire time, and two tried "traying" down a hillside a couple of times before giving up.

At least none of us got frostbite?

CODY

When I'm planning a game, I have a tendency to take an otherwise simple idea and make it way bigger and better (or just grosser). That's how my summer camp game of Ultimate Frisbee turned into Ultimate Fishbee. Yes, that means we threw a fish across a field like a frisbee. First we tried a salmon, but learned salmon falls apart when thrown. Too flaky. Next we tried a frozen tilapia.

I first noticed we had a problem when I caught the tilapia after a long pass. Ouch! Those frozen scales hurt! My hand was bleeding a little bit, but we were nearly halfway through the game, so I decided to suck it up. When the half was called and we walked off the field for a break, I noticed that nearly ten of my students' hands were bleeding too.

That's when one of my freshman guys showed me his finger. A spine from the fish had impaled it. The spine had entered through the pad of his finger and had pierced his fingernail. Understandably, he was a little freaked out. As we walked off the field to rinse his wound in a water fountain, the reality of his injury started to set in. The poor kid got queasy, fell, and hit his head on the metal water fountain. We picked him up, carried him to a car, headed for the hospital, and called the boy's parents on the way.

Twenty minutes after we arrived at the hospital and got the kid his first set of X-rays, my phone rang. It was a parent asking why her son was in the hospital . . . but not the parent I had spoken to. I assumed the camp nurse had made a mistake, so I promised I'd call her right back after I had sorted it out.

After a few phone calls, I learned what had happened. Twenty minutes after we had left for the hospital, a couple of other boys were messing around. A six-foot senior guy had jumped onto the back of a freshman guy, knocking him to the ground and spraining his back, making it difficult for him to breathe. He arrived at the hospital a few minutes later.

Happily, both students left the hospital that night, neither injury was serious, and all was well. But oh boy, please never throw a frozen fish at teenagers.

MATTHEW

I recently took a group of students on a five-hour trip to a conference in another city. On our way home, I was pretty exhausted, so I stopped at a gas station, grabbed a coffee, and started to fill up on gas. I was having some trouble getting the nozzle to fit into the gas tank, but I made it work and hit the road.

A few minutes later, we heard strange sounds and saw smoke pouring out of our exhaust. That's when I realized . . . the nozzle hadn't fit into my gas tank because it was the diesel nozzle. I had just filled our 15-passenger van with diesel fuel. This happened the same day AAA's computer system was down nationwide, so we had to find a rental van instead of getting our van repaired. When we finally hit the road (again), one of my students opened the glove compartment of the rental van and *found a gun.* Obviously, we had to return that vehicle.

We finally got everything straightened out, but I will forever bear the nickname, "Van Diesel."

Here's a story about my youth pastor (who is now my lead pastor). When I was in high school, our youth group did an annual Valentine's Day breakfast. Each year, the guys and girls would take turns planning it. During one of the guys' turns to play the breakfast, we decided to dress up as superheroes while we cooked.

Not surprisingly, our cooking set off the fire alarm. The kitchen filled with smoke, the alarm blared, and soon the fire department showed up in the church parking lot. As they arrived, my youth pastor flung open the kitchen door and ran into the parking lot, yelling, "It's okay! Everything is okay!"

He was still wearing his skin-tight full-body Batman costume.

CHAD

After several years serving as a missionary in another country, I finally took a job as a youth pastor and moved back to the US. One evening, some of my students invited me to see a movie with them. Having just moved back to the country, I hadn't heard anything about the movie they wanted to see, but I was up for it.

The first few minutes of the movie had me laughing hysterically, but after about twenty minutes it started to get pretty raunchy.

At that point, I didn't know what to do. Should I leave? (I was their youth pastor, after all.) Should I stay? (The movie was really funny.)

It's not my finest moment, but I did decide to stay. I definitely got a word from my senior pastor about it, but wow, that movie made me laugh.

JOHNATHAN

We were playing volleyball one night at youth group with some pretty decent players. Since everyone playing had some talent, we could at least set and spike enough to have a little fun. Plus, spiking the ball at a high school kid always makes me feel pretty good about myself.

That's when one of my leaders set me up for a beautiful spike. I went in for the kill.

But as my elbow came backward, I felt it make contact with something. I heard a pop. When I turned around, there was a kid lying in a bloody heap on the ground beside me. I had broken his nose with my elbow.

I felt bad for a second, but then I realized he hadn't even been playing volleyball with us! He had run onto the court right in the middle of the game! Who does that?

AUSTIN

One week, I called an all-girls round for one of our games because our boys had been trying to play (and dominate) every single round. For the all-girls round, I sent all the guys to the back of the room to watch while the girls played.

Just before we started to play, I noticed a guy had snuck into the girls' group, so I called him out. I told him to head back with the guys, but he didn't move. I was pretty ticked that this kid was messing with me, so I said into the microphone, "Dude, you're the ugliest girl I've ever seen. Go join the guys!" I was so mad.

The kid left the girls' team . . . and ran into the girls' bathroom. Still oblivious, I sent a leader to go into the bathroom and pull him out of there. "There are no guys in there," my leader told me. "Just the girl that you called ugly."

So, uh . . . is anyone hiring?

ALISHA

Our church has a huge empty field that hardly ever gets used, so I decided to give it some purpose. How? I planned a giant food fight.

First, we called a local grocery store and asked for all of their rotten food. We loaded all of it into my truck, headed back to the church, and gave it all a brief inspection to make sure there wasn't anything deadly in it. After a full afternoon of sorting through heaps of mold and rotting food, we invited our students to the most epic food fight of all time.

Looking back, we probably should have done this during the light of day. At night, in the dark, things didn't go very well. Several kids took potatoes to the face. Others twisted their ankles in holes in the ground they couldn't see. One kid got hit in the back with an enormous cheese log.

Next time, I think we'll stick to water fights. In the daylight.

KODY

One summer, I led a high school mission trip to Honduras. During some free time one afternoon, I took our students to the public zoo. It just so happened that we walked by the monkey exhibit just as feeding time was beginning.

Apparently they do zoos a little differently in Honduras because this monkey exhibit had an opening for the monkeys to go in and out of their enclosure. As we passed by, a monkey jumped out of its exhibit, leaped onto a fence post directly in front of me, and tried to slap me across the face.

He missed me, but then he went after my students and latched onto the shorts of one of our girls, screaming, and jumping up and down.

I managed to pull her from the monkey's clutches, but she's been terrified of monkeys ever since.

One Sunday as we began our service, a kid threw a pen at me while I was on stage. I mean, he really zinged it.

And I caught it! Honestly, it was pretty impressive. The entire room collectively said, "Whoooooooaaaaaa!" and some people even clapped.

Thinking about my movie hero Jason Bourne, I said, "I got these reflexes from watching so much Bourne!"

Unfortunately, everyone thought I said "porn."

It was our first year leading a small group and my husband and I were so excited. We'd recently moved back to our hometown and were eager to get involved with the high school ministry. When we received our small group roster, we recognized a few names, but not everyone.

When the night came for our first small group meeting at our house, we were so excited to meet them and make a good impression.

One of my girls was named Emma and I knew her family was hosting a foreign exchange student that semester, so when Emma walked in accompanied by an Asian girl I had never met before, I said confidently (and a little slowly), "Hello, you must be Emma's foreign exchange student!"

"Uh, no, I'm Jade," she said. The foreign exchange student hadn't arrived yet.

LISA

I was one month into my tenure as a youth pastor and was trying to be intentional about connecting with my students whenever possible.

One day, I was thrilled to receive a text message from one of my students! She was asking a simple question about how to turn in a form for an upcoming event, but I decided to spin it into a longer conversation.

When she told me about her recent cheerleading competition, I intended to respond with, "FUN!"

Instead, I sent, "FU."

BRETT

We've all had moments when we've gotten a little tongue-tied while we were teaching. You might remember that poor sap who said, "they pinched their tits" instead of, "they pitched their tents." That moment was pretty bad. But mine was worse.

It's as simple and as terrible as this. I was teaching a room of one hundred students and thirty volunteers about nothing less than the life-changing Gospel of Jesus Christ. It was a big deal. I was so intent on sharing with this room who Jesus was and what His death and resurrection means for us, that . . . well, I guess I stumbled over my words.

Because, ladies and gentlemen, I didn't actually say the "resurrection" of our Lord and Savior Jesus Christ.

I said His "erection."

You're welcome. Now please forget you ever read this story.

That's the end of this book, but the stories
and conversation don't need to end here.
Come join the Stuff You Can Use youth
ministry community on Facebook, where this
whole idea began. We'd love to have you!

STUFFYOUCANUSE.ORG/COMMUNITY

CURRICULUM AND ANNUAL STRATEGY

DISCIPLESHIP **TEACHING** **GAMES**

EVENTS **VOLUNTEERS** **PARENTS**

"Grow is a game-changing resource that provides a strategy to every aspect of my ministry!"
— CORY (Summerville, SC)

GROWCURRICULUM.ORG

ELLE & KENNY CAMPBELL

Kenny and Elle were youth pastors in Buffalo, NY (home of the chicken finger sub) for almost ten years. Kenny was the Middle School Pastor and Elle was the Small Groups and Volunteer Coordinator for Middle School Ministry. While they were there, they founded Stuff You Can Use (stuffyoucanuse.org), a youth ministry resource company, as a way to share the resources they were already creating for their ministry with others.

Today, Kenny and Elle live in Atlanta, GA, where they lead the Stuff You Can Use team full-time, host the podcast Youth Ministry Answers, coach and train youth workers around the country, and serve students and small group leaders every Sunday as youth ministry volunteers.

When Kenny and Elle aren't creating youth ministry resources, they're usually playing games, listening to podcasts, exploring new cities, and looking for things that make them laugh.